STOPPING OUT

A GUIDE TO
LEAVING COLLEGE
AND GETTING BACK IN

Judi R. Kesselman

M. EVANS & COMPANY, INC.
New York, N.Y. 10017

For every mom and dad,
and especially mine.

M. Evans and Company titles are distributed in
the United States by the J. B. Lippincott Company,
East Washington Square, Philadelphia, Pa. 19105;
and in Canada by McClelland & Stewart Ltd.,
25 Hollinger Road, Toronto M4B 3G2, Ontario

LIBRARY OF CONGRESS CATALOGING IN PUBLICATION DATA
Kesselman, Judi R
  Stopping out, a guide to leaving college and getting back in.
  Bibliography: p.
  Includes index.
  1. College dropouts. 2. College attendance. I. Title.
LC148.K47   378.1'69'13   76-1906
ISBN 0-87131-199-2
ISBN 0-87131-209-3 pbk.

Design by Joel Schick

Manufactured in the United States of America

9 8 7 6 5 4 3 2 1

STOPPING OUT

Contents

Acknowledgments

I am especially indebted to the Carnegie Commission on Higher Education and the Task Force on Higher Education (the Newman Commission) for their recognition of the stopout phenomenon, and to the few people—notably Dean K. Whitla and Nancy Silver Lindsay at Harvard University, Larry J. Yartz at Allegheny College, and C. Hess Haagen at Wesleyan University in Connecticut—who have attempted to compile information on the stopout. From these studies in particular emerged the portrait of the stopout which my own interviews were able to corroborate, and which is reproduced throughout this book.

I want to thank the approximately eighty students across the country whose candid comments were so helpful—and particularly those whose representative accounts appear in their own words throughout the book.

I am also grateful to all the college presidents, deans, and admissions officers who accepted telephone calls and found time for personal interviews.

For information on the colleges' attitudes and policies with regard to stopouts, I received assistance from 101 colleges, out of 225 to whom I addressed a survey questionnaire. (The colleges were selected from *Barron's Profile of American Colleges* so as to include in greater proportion the schools that attract the most student interest; I queried all the schools listed as "most competitive," 90 percent of those called "highly competitive," 60 percent of those listed as "competitive," and nine schools from the very large "less competitive" list.)

The people at the College Entrance Examination Board graciously opened their files and tracked down obscure booklets for me. Dr. Alexander Astin provided warm encouragement. And Professor Robert Cope went out of his way to extend his hand to a stranger across three thousand miles; words can't express my appreciation for his help.

In addition, my thanks to the research librarians at the Great Neck Public Library: Sue Weiland, Arlene Warshaw, Elsa Resnick, Carol Miller, Susan Dudleson, Charles Buckley, and Dorothy Tulman.

And to my editor, Nancy Uberman, for unrelentingly insisting on first-best. And to Joe Kesselman for his editorial suggestions and hand-holding; and to our sons for putting up with a nearly empty refrigerator and overflowing clothes hamper for eight long months. And to Jon Mendelson, without whom this book would never have been conceived.

1

What
Is
Stopping
Out?

IT was June 1744. The commissioners of the British colonies of Maryland and Virginia were meeting with the leaders of six Indian nations to sign the Treaty of Lancaster. At the meeting, the Virginians made a magnanimous gesture of friendship: they invited the Indians to send six of their sons to the second New World college, William and Mary.

The Indians refused the offer. "We know," they answered politely, "that you highly esteem the kind of learning taught in those colleges, and that the maintenance of our young men, while with you, would be very expensive to you. We are convinced, therefore, that you mean to do us good by your proposal, and we thank you heartily. But you, who are wise, must know that different nations have different conceptions of things; and therefore not take it amiss, if our ideas of this kind of education happen not to be the same with yours. We have had some experience of it; several of our young people were formerly brought up at the colleges of the northern provinces; they were instructed in all your sciences; but when they came back to us they were bad runners, ignorant of every means of living in the woods, unable to bear cold or hunger, knew neither how to build a cabin, take a deer, nor kill an enemy, spoke our language imperfectly, were therefore neither fit for hunters, warriors nor counsellors; they were totally good for nothing. We are however not the less obliged by your kind offer, though we decline accepting it; and, to show our grateful sense of it, if the gentlemen of Virginia will send us a dozen of their sons, we will take great care of their education, instruct them in all we know, and make *men* of them."

—Recorded by
BENJAMIN FRANKLIN

Many people today—undergraduates and, increasingly, administrators—agree with those Indians. They are questioning closely the expensive educational structure which, while instructing students in the abstract arts and sciences, often graduates them unprepared for life in the everyday world. While they don't question the fact that a college degree is often prerequisite to future success, they are beginning to recognize that some kinds of important learning occur only outside the sheltered campus. This year more than 50 percent of all undergraduates will be leaving school to seek this learning.

But of that 50 percent, only a small minority can be considered dropouts. Studies at Princeton indicated that 70 percent of their students who drop out come back to get their degrees. Research at the University of Illinois produced almost identical results. And a 1971 survey of colleges throughout the nation reported that, of a 53 percent dropout population, 84 percent fully expect to get the B.A.—and 51 percent plan graduate degrees. These figures support a reality that the general educational community is only beginning to identify and deal with: that most of the dropouts among college students are merely *stopouts,* and that among them are America's brightest and most promising scholars.

These stopout students include the thinkers, the nonconformists, the innovators. They insist that, while the conventional four-year undergraduate pattern is viable for many, it is not the *only* possible pattern, or even, for them, the best. They withdraw for a semester or more to work, to travel, to study independently, to do some thinking. Then, when they've found what they need outside academia, they return to finish college.

Stopping out is not new. But until a few years ago it was never understood by academic authorities because it was never distinguished from dropping out. Every study of students who left college failed to separate the ones who shouldn't have been there in the first place, or the ones who had taken as much education as they needed or wanted, from the far larger group who fully expected to return to college. Then, in 1971, two prestigious commissions officially separated the stopouts from the dropouts.

The first research group to define the stopout—indeed,

to invent the very word—was the Carnegie Commission on Higher Education, which was funded by the Carnegie Corporation. Under the chairmanship of Clark Kerr, and utilizing the talents of some of the most creative and innovative thinkers in higher education today, the commission issued no less than eighty landmark reports in its five years of existence. But its greatest achievement by far was to spotlight and endorse this rapidly growing student practice of taking time out.

The second group was the Task Force on Higher Education, funded by the Ford Foundation under the auspices of the Office of Education of the Department of Health, Education and Welfare. Its findings—volume one issued in 1971 and volume two in 1974—are collectively referred to as the Newman Report, after the group's chairman, Frank Newman. The report supported the concepts that college education needn't be fitted into four consecutive years and that most students could actually benefit from a stop-out, stop-in pattern of education.

Publication of these two reports has caused a quiet revolution in academic circles. In colleges across the country, researchers have begun to study *stopouts*. Their conclusion: that students are viewing college not as a bastion of culture and tradition but as a marketable commodity—an *expensive* one. The student acts as consumer, buying and paying for specific goods and services; therefore he selects carefully, and not necessarily all at once. College administrators have begun to heed the researchers' reports and to recognize the legitimacy of this alternative view of education.

As mentioned before, the actual practice of stopping out

is not new. It can be traced far back to before the Depression of the thirties—although in those days people stopped out for mostly financial reasons. At that time, college was mainly for acculturation; it was considered a necessity only for professionals: teachers, doctors, lawyers, engineers. Back in 1900, college was nearly always the next step for high school graduates—but there were few high school graduates. After the First World War, many more students graduated from high school, but the proportion who went on to college greatly dropped.

In truly aspiring families it became common for a young man, if he showed "promise," to work a few years after high school to save the money to "put himself through college." But for the vast majority, higher education remained a luxury item.

During the Depression, there occurred a subtle shift in the advantages of higher education. As unemployment rates soared, the college degree suddenly tended to give its holder a competitive edge for that copyboy job on the *Daily News,* or the floorwalker job at Macy's. College was no longer the means of acquiring culture and a profession, but a ticket to employment in an era of joblessness.

Then came the Second World War, and after it that great leveler, the GI Bill. Young men and women, after seeing the advantages of a college degree during the Depression, flocked to academia with Uncle Sam often footing the bill. And after earning their own degrees, they vowed that their children would enter the marketplace similarly equipped. From the forties to the seventies, popular advice was "Get that paper and you'll get that job." We had entered the age of education for certification, out of the long era of education for culture which had begun in America before the United States was born. Suddenly, staying in college insured one's future. Dropping out, to parents and educators who'd formed their ideas in the thirties, meant never going back. Without any new statistical evidence, this conclusion—which had once been irrefutable—was still accepted as hard fact.

By the late fifties and the sixties, higher education for all had become a national obsession. Parents clamored to get their sons and daughters into college. The more prosperous economy put higher education into a sellers' market. Community colleges were built to meet the demand, opening at the startling rate of one per week. Universities expanded campuses and quickly erected new dormitories, just as they had responded with quonset huts to meet the housing demands for the returning GIs of 1946.

With the public placing such a premium on higher education, dropping out was viewed with disapproval. The college dropout was stigmatized along with high school dropouts, and no distinction was made between the two groups.

The administrators on the college campuses were also guilty of dropout-aversion. Generally, their attitude toward the ex-students was one of "good riddance." Their offices of institutional research developed studies that tagged these people "academic failures." Statistical reports dealt with "attrition," with "withdrawal," with "failure to complete a four-year degree program," all indiscriminate terms.

Researchers were interested mainly in the problems "attrition" generated for the campus administrators. Schools were spending between two hundred and five hundred dollars per student trying to attract them onto campus— plus the time and money invested in teaching, advising, record-keeping, housing, scholarships, loans, work-study programs. One report candidly explained, "Each dropout represents a loss to the institution of not only a place which may have been taken up by another person able to complete the program of instruction, but also a wide-ranging set of academic resources invested in [him]." Thus, the four-year graduate was a credit, an alumnus, a representative of the school; the nongraduate was an embarrassment, a monetary liability. So when an enrolled student left, he was seldom thought of again.

In the late fifties and sixties, there were always more applicants than places on campus. Even the smallest, least known college was turning away prospective students. In 1972, educational researcher Dyckman W. Vermilye was predicting that by the year 2000 between 75 and 90 percent of all American youth would be attending college at some point in their lives. There were no indications that schools would ever have a shortage of applicants.

Then came the recession, and the predictions of continuing expansion had to be considered in a new light. The Carnegie Commission, in its report *Priorities for Action*, announced, "We were among the first to call attention several years ago to the 1980s as a 'stop' period after a century when enrollments had doubled every 10 to 15 years. But we did not anticipate that the declining rate of enrollment increases would occur so soon and so fast in the 1970s or that the 1980s might turn out to be such a period of continuing slow growth."

The first colleges to find themselves suddenly without enough applicants to take the places of the "failures" and "withdrawals" were the smaller, lesser known private liberal arts colleges—schools like Beaver in Philadelphia, Salem in West Virginia, and Loretto Heights in Denver. In 1973–74, two dozen overexpanded colleges closed, while others began to cut back their faculties. Admissions officers had to try a new approach: hard-sell recruitment.

A number of schools began to offer cash payments and tuition rebates to enrolled students who recruited friends for the school. Merit scholars were enticed with full-tuition scholarships because their attendance, the schools believed, might attract other students to the campus. College fairs toured from town to town, with booths manned by admissions people. One booth offered jelly beans, another free shopping bags—all in addition to full-color filmstrips, brochures, and peptalks. All these efforts were devoted to one end—to get written expressions of interest onto little file cards, together with names, addresses, and phone numbers of prospective students. The admission officers would then contact these people with more literature, and encourage them to apply.

Some people, like Richard Moll, admissions director of Bowdoin, stopped to wonder if the boat-show atmosphere was appropriate for the college search. But voices which, like his, came from schools that were still attracting a plenitude of applicants, were in the minority.

Admissions management firms proliferated, offering higher education their advertising expertise; a number of schools signed contracts turning over the student recruitment job to these salesmen. Charles Marshall, assistant executive director of the National Association of College Admissions Counselors and himself an organizer of college fairs, admitted, "There's always been competition for the top athletes and the best scholars, but now it's simply a matter of keeping the classes filled and surviving."

By 1974, expensive private colleges and even public universities were beginning to feel the pinch. State colleges experienced their first overall decline in first-year students in many years. The prestigious northeast colleges counted fifteen thousand vacancies. Contrary to all predictions of the sixties, applications from minority students fell in number. Perhaps this was due to a disillusionment with higher education as a stepladder to economic and social opportunities—by the mid-seventies the labor force had contracted and there were too many people with college degrees in the job market.Those with postgraduate educations were often "overqualified" for the available jobs, and those with B.A.s were a glut on the market. Apprenticeship in trades, the *New York Times* reported, had a somewhat greater effect in raising earnings than did college education.

Despite the fact that a college education no longer guarantees job opportunities, to many it is still an asset worth pursuing. Most students who start college and then leave to try to get jobs are finding that doors are closed unless they have a degree. Although more and more *seem* to be dropping out all the time, the Carnegie and Newman commissions have pointed out that these students are not permanent dropouts. After a year or two

of a breather, most of them find out that they need higher
education to achieve their goals. The fact is, 85 percent
of the people who start college eventually get their
degrees.

With the general decline in applicants, some forward-
thinking college administrators have begun to focus on
their stopouts. If they are leaving campus anyway, the
reasoning goes, why not let them leave with good wishes,
encouragement, even approval? If they depart with good
feeling, perhaps they will return to their home campus
when the stopout is over.

The Carnegie Commission consolidated and legitimized
this positive point of view by inventing the word *stopout*.
In their first research report, released in 1971, it was
recommended that young people be *given* time to stop
out from college, or between high school and college,
to work or study or just discover their own reasons for
going to school.

When the commission reported that as many ex-stopouts seemed to be going on to graduate school as the
"persisters"—the students who could be relied on to remain
at one college for four straight years—their evidence did
much to undo the traditional bias against the stopout. The
leave of absence, a mechanism originally provided for
students with low marks, health problems, or financial
reverses, was modernized in many schools to attract the
new leave-takers. The deferred admission, which had
been introduced partly to guarantee a place to draftees
during the Korean and Vietnam wars, was broadened
to include prospective students who had other "extenuat-
ing circumstances" for putting off college. The acceptable

reasons for obtaining a leave or deferral varied greatly from campus to campus. (In fact, there was—and still is—at many schools an understandable reluctance to suggest the availability of these options.) But mechanisms for stopping out now exist at most schools.

The chapters that follow will identify all the options now available, where they can be found, and how the student can use them to get the most out of college. True, some schools embrace innovation quickly, and other schools proceed at a slower pace. But most are beginning to recognize that the stopout is a searcher, not a failure; they are beginning to cater to his needs, not only when he's on his way out but also when he returns.

2

Who Stops Out and Why?

Aт Adelphi we used to conduct interviews as a matter of course with students considering leaving school. The number if students dropping out has increased so much, we don't have the staff any more.

—HAROLD GAINER, Director of Faculty Advisers, Adelphi University*

To answer adequately the question, "Who stops out?" we must first know who today's students are. They are, by upbringing, far removed from the college students of the twenties, the thirties, and the forties. Economically, they belong to a generation born during a relatively affluent

* Quoted in a *Newsday* article by David Behrens.

period. Socially, they reached adolescence two to three years sooner than their parents did, in generally more permissive homes. Their channels of information were widened by the advent of television and new, widespread modes of travel. Their earlier adolescence, coupled with a later maturity delayed by long years of education, produced a gap which resulted in the creation of a new intermediate growth stage which has been documented by sociologist Kenneth Keniston in his numerous books and articles. He uses the term *youth* in referring to this level of development.

The distinguishing characteristic of youth, says Keniston, is not rebellion—which these students left behind years ago—but investigation. They seek to understand who they are—their social roles, their vocations, their relationships to the existing society. Through probing the realities of adult life, and through constant self-scrutiny as they experiment with role after role, they are slowly developing a selfhood which may be very different from the sense of identity their parents inherited from their own parents, and from the generation before them.

Their main characteristic, says Keniston, is the need to be in a state of flux. In *The American Scholar*, he states, "Youth grows panicky when confronted with the feeling of 'getting nowhere,' of 'being stuck in a rut,' or of 'not moving.' Youth holds the assumption that to 'grow up' is in some ultimate sense to cease to be really alive." That restless quality characteristic of youth leads many to drop out of school. And when they've "found themselves," more than two-thirds of the dropouts stop in again.

How Many Students Really Do Stop Out?

Although statistics on the subject have been compiled by academic investigators, nobody really knows how many students stop out during any given time, from any given school. Until recently, nearly every study of college dropouts included the students who flunked out, the ones who had never intended to graduate, those who transferred directly to other schools, and those who took official leaves of absence. Some researchers suggest that all these figures reflect only the tip of the iceberg. But even recent studies have discounted the many students who leave between semesters without notifying the school, or the deferred-admission students whose numbers have grown perceptibly in the last five years.

Although the statistics are far from complete, they offer two conclusions. First, that the number of dropouts has remained close to about 50 percent for the past fifty years. Secondly, many of these dropouts are really *stop-outs*—students who are merely taking a break, for various reasons, before going back to get a degree.

A 1971 nationwide study by Alexander Astin for the American Council on Education revealed that of 25,000 four-year-college freshmen in 1961, only 47 percent graduated four years later. Of those who had dropped out, 84 percent fully expected eventually to get their degrees and 51 percent anticipated going to graduate schools. A 1963 University of Illinois study showed that 70 percent of its dropouts had achieved their bachelor's degrees within ten years. And one Arizona university, which once traced all its former students, discovered that most of them graduated—there or elsewhere—up to thirty years later.

What Kinds of Students Stop Out?

What characterizes the stopouts? Can they be distinguished from the rest of the undergraduate community *before* they leave?

After many years of trying to predict which students are potential stopouts—in order to admit instead students who are likely to remain for four years—most college researchers have abandoned the effort. Their unsuccessful attempts only emphasize the lack of obvious differences in scholastic performance between the stopout and the stay-in. The stopout's grades and attendance record are as good or even slightly better; and his Scholastic Aptitude Test scores and high school marks are not differentiating factors.

There is one distinguishing feature: the stopout usually has less financial aid, and seldom is one of the less-privileged minority students. Studies indicate that most disadvantaged college students, if they leave school, do so out of economic necessity; as a group, those who stay get their degrees in four straight years.

Several studies have attempted to sketch a profile of the stopout personality. From these studies, the stopout appears to be more stubborn, assertive, skeptical, and independent than the stay-in, who is described as essentially accepting and conforming. The stopout's thinking shows an abstract, theoretical bent. He critically analyzes himself and his environment, supports social change, and experiences feelings of anxiety and alienation. Yet he readily tolerates the discomfort that accompanies a life-style based on questioning.

In contrast, the stay-in is a realistic, materialistic person who adapts, socializes, and perseveres. His life-style is at equilibrium. He lacks the flexibility of the stopout, and tends to be upset by changes.

The stopout is disturbing to have around (or stimulating, depending upon the point of view taken), because he challenges the system. Counselors refer to him in their reports as "mixed-up, troublesome." But this type of student also tends to be creative, as attested to by educator Paul Heist's book, *The Creative College Student: An Unmet Challenge.*

Of course, these are all generalizations, these traits which belong to the "typical" stopout personality. There are far too few reliable personality correlates to enable researchers to use this profile to predict the potential stopout.

Why Do Students Stop Out?

Stopouts leave for one of several reasons—none of which fits neatly into the three little boxes, financial, personal, or academic, provided by most exit interview forms under the heading "reason for leaving school." The real causes often have to do with the student's expectations about college, as well as with his feelings about himself. Sometimes, however, stopping out is not his best solution to a problem; he might do better simply by transferring to another school, or seeking new options at his present school. Sometimes, a stopout should be a dropout—perhaps formal education does not meet his needs.

Stopouts Whose Reasons Make Good Sense

Before the sixties, the major reasons for taking a leave of absence were marriage, full-time job offers, intimate family crises, or illness. In the late sixties, fewer students left for those reasons, while more stopped out to express their dissatisfaction with a rigidly structured educational community. By the seventies, the trend had changed once again. These students now keep in mind that, despite its faults, college means certification and increased earning potential. So they work within the system, often despite outside commitments, as long as they feel they are getting what they came to college for. It's when their personal goals are unclear, or not in accord with academia's, that they decide to stop out.

Sometimes they express it as a "need to get my head together," or a desire to "do something real for a while." The majority of stopouts leave for one of these two personal reasons.

1. Wanting to Do Nonacademic Things

Some students stop out simply because they want to experiment with other kinds of situations. They stop out to teach themselves new skills or knowledge, or to pursue their current educational goals through an apprenticeship, a job, or a correspondence course. Within this group, a number will discover that they don't need a formal college setting to attain their goals. The rest, though, will eventually return to school after their stop-outs.

Sometimes, according to new research by Dr. C. Hess Haagen,* students leave specifically *because* of a high degree of academic involvement, and the need to pursue it in off-campus work. They stop out to test their goals —and to enrich their programs with experience. For example, science people may stop out to test whether they are interested in research or medicine, or to find out what is really expected of them in industry. A common question, no matter what the major, is, "I know I can do the academics, but can I succeed in the real world?" Stopping out may provide the answer.

Some students stop out because they know they don't belong in college right now. While their intellects have raced ahead, their social growth kept slower pace. They need some time to catch up emotionally. (More and more, they're deciding to take time off before they even start college. The percentage entering directly from high school went from 63 percent in 1968 to 53 percent in 1972.)

A good many students know they don't belong in college now because their grades have not met their own, or the school's, standards. Frequently these students stay in school because they're afraid that if they stop studying they'll forget how. The opposite seems true: most of the

---

* Dr. Haagen is conducting the first multicollege long-term study on stopouts.

deans and admissions officers who responded to my questionnaire indicated—often with backup statistics—that stopouts earn *better* grades when they return to education. At Lindenwood College in Missouri, for example, students' post-stopout averages went up by one full grade.

2. Wanting to Get in Touch with Their Goals

Many students I spoke to had left school expressly to learn who *they* were, as much as to learn what the world was all about. They wanted to make mistakes and grow from the consequences; they wanted to produce tangible achievements and grow from the pleasure. They wanted the beginnings of self-fulfillment.

These students fully expected to go back to school full of purpose, eager to work toward achievement of their professional ambitions. Most found they were reaching for traditional goals; they were looking to find their fulfillment within society's framework.

> *Now that I've tried a few things on my own, I need the expert advice that's available to me on campus. But I couldn't take advantage of it until I knew what questions to ask.*
>
> —GLENN ZAGORIN

Many students stop out, once they get to college, because it's the first time they can make an independent move without directly confronting their parents' expectations. Parental influence can be overwhelming while a person is living at home, but it can't always sustain its force across all the miles between home and campus. With some, the drive to become independent overshadows their scholastic motivation. When their grades nose-dive, they recognize that they need time to find themselves and to develop genuine motivation toward their studies. They speak of personal growth, of finding direction, of getting in touch with a deeper sense of self.

Very much akin to these stopouts are the ones who had concentrated for so long on getting the grades for college that they never thought, "What am I going for?" until they arrived. A clear sense of purpose will strengthen motivation; but a lack of direction will undermine a student's ability to push through coursework. Students who lose interest in school—often with an accompanying dip in grades—often recognize that a stopout will be the only thing that will restore their enthusiasm for college. Behind such reasoning may be the intention of getting into graduate school, and an awareness of the admissions premium placed on top grades. Stopouts have been shown to restore the enthusiasm—and improve the grades.

A 1970 survey of flunk-outs, reported by Pitcher and Blauschild, pointed to one cause of failing grades: "It is difficult to be motivated to a goal that one does not have the aptitude for, or wants for either reasons of parent-approval or parent-rejection." Yet that is how many career choices are initially made. How do students discover and develop a career goal of their own? The Newman Report recognizes: "We doubt whether many students have had sufficient exposure outside the educational system to know what a relevant education might be. Both students and faculty need more experiences away from the campus."

Closely associated with the need to find a direction before continuing college is the need to answer "Why college anyway?" In an Oswego College dropout study, students who checked "dissatisfaction" as their reason for leaving school were encouraged to be more specific. Many answered that they were unable to see how college related to their personal goals and aspirations, or to see how their investment of time and money would produce tangible returns. Robert E. Schell, assistant dean of students and author of the report, concluded that students who transfer to other schools often do so because of this very pertinent "dissatisfaction." Usually, however, a transfer won't solve the problem, whereas a stopout spent in reevaluation and redefinition of goals probably will.

Stopouts Who Need a Transfer

There are occasions when the situation is reversed: many stop out, when all they need is a transfer. Included in this group is the large number of students who leave disappointed with the college they've entered.

Choosing a college can be like buying property "sight unseen." And often the process of selection is based on superficial or incorrect impressions. The advice of high school counselors cannot always be relied on, since advisers cannot be well informed about the more than two thousand colleges. The colleges themselves cannot supply objective information since they are, after all, in the business of selling education. So it is the buyer's prerogative—indeed, his duty—to consider quality, fit, and style in making his choice.

The "fit" of a school should be an all-important consideration. A small-college student in a large school, a technically minded person in a liberal arts setting, an intellectual in a low-pressure school, a straight-thinker on an experimental campus—each will find that his values and life-style will differ from those of the majority of other students on the campus. Almost inevitably, he will leave that college. "If there is friction between the person and the place," educator Robert Cope said, "it is the person who inevitably wears away."

I applied to Shimer because I wanted a small school after my enormous high school. I didn't know until I got there that there might be such a thing as getting to know other kids too well.

—ELIZABETH WALLERSTEIN

They said they were nonsectarian and that chapel was optional, but when I got there I discovered that most of the students were the chapel-going type. We never could connect in our attitudes.

—JOHN BERLE

The school was played up as being innovative. Once there I discovered it was as rigid in its innovations as other schools were in their traditions.

—SALLY TIMKINS

Leaving one's first college is becoming more prevalent every year. A 1969 study of 146 colleges reported that while in 1966 roughly one transfer student had been admitted for every four freshmen, the projected ratio for 1974 was one to one. Recent surveys seem to have borne out the prediction and in some cases even to have surpassed it.

Many students recognize immediately that they're in the wrong school and promptly take steps to transfer out. But the number of people asking for direct transfers has been decreasing, while a larger number decides to stop out to look for alternate schools. While investigating a school that looks promising, they spend a week or a month on the campus, perhaps even taking a course or two before officially enrolling. In general whether to stop out first or to transfer immediately should depend on how much you really know about that second school.

Another situation in which a transfer may remedy the problem is the one in which there's pressure to choose a major. Relatively few students stop out who are committed, right from the first semester, to one major. Many students will stop out if they feel pushed by their college to choose a major before they're ready. These are the students who either were working so hard in high school that they never stopped to consider long-range goals or the ones who thought they had a definite goal until they discovered, in college, that there are hundreds of degree majors—and in many schools the additional freedom to combine majors or create new ones. Being required to narrow down can be a problem, especially for the perceptive student who realizes that he has little conception of what most of these majors mean out in the real world.

But some schools permit their students to defer the choice of major almost indefinitely, and others have new programs in which students can sample several majors before they have to make a final choice. So for the student who is undecided about a major, perhaps all that is needed is a transfer to one of these schools.

Stopouts Who Should Stay Where They Are

Although many educators feel strongly that a stopout can be an enriching experience for almost everybody, some students use it to escape the realities of dogma, structure, and impersonalism found on almost every college campus. Eventually, if they want the degree, they'll have to accept these shortcomings.

The shortcomings are considerable, too. In its report *Priorities for Action,* the Carnegie Commission rated higher education's performance over the past few decades. " 'General education,' " it wrote, "began to decay on many campuses and nothing was put in its place. Standards of teaching were often sacrificed to other activities. The colleges seemed intent upon processing more and more graduates, almost without regard to the general or specific needs of society, as in the case of the surplus of Ph.D.'s. . . . Higher education, on occasion, even seemed to have lost faith in the mind."

In addition, many colleges are rife with bureaucratic rules and regulations which seem set up simply to frustrate the more individualistic students. Professor Cope has himself bemoaned the "excessive demands to fill out the proper form at the appointed time and leave it with the correct office." Although it's rarely enough in itself to make a student stop out, it's often the scale-tipping factor.

Then there are the classes—the nub of education—which often turn out to be empty of substance. For the bright students from suburban schools, there is swift disillusionment. ("For English and languages, my high school was better," one stopout commented.) Courses seem to offer, in most cases, preparation for nothing but other courses. Textbooks often contain material that seems irrelevant to the student. Subject matter is mired in minutiae. "They [the students] merely examine in excruciating detail perhaps 0.00001 of the world—the rest they'll have to learn on their own. It's a ridiculous definition of higher education," wrote educator Alexander Mood.

Courses are still being taught mainly with a lecture-hall approach, especially in the universities. For those students who've been learning-by-doing since nursery school, the fact that higher education hasn't caught up with modern educational theories is usually quite a shock. "Passive note-taking learning," says Dr. Mood, "is not very appropriate for persons beyond the age of twelve." When, at age eighteen, a student finds he has to settle for the inflexible information that is dispensed dogmatically in the classroom, he thinks about stopping out.

The thought would less often result in the action if faculty were more approachable and supportive. But all too often, they're distant and impersonal. For creativity to emerge, the student *needs* a good relationship with his teacher; instead there is frequently a void which the bright undergraduate fills quickly with the realization that to the professors he's a cipher—an A or a C.

Nonetheless, Wesleyan researcher Dr. Haagen told me that his staff had interviewed a good many students who had taken official leaves of absence—and relatively few said they had left solely because of poor teaching or bureaucratic administration. The few who did were faced with a problem that stopping out could not solve directly. The fact remained: to get the degree, the drawbacks inherent in college have to be coped with and endured.

Stopouts Whose Stated Reason May Not Be the Real Reasons

Sometimes stopouts check off "financial" as the reason for their leaves, when their real reasons have little to do with actual lack of money. They may really be in the wrong college, in which case they're saying, "The program at this school is not worth the price." Or they may be redefining their goals and feelings, as many stopouts expressed to me, "If I don't know where I'm going, why am I spending such an enormous amount of my parents' money in the meantime?" Reconsidering what they mean by "financial," enables students to take the most appropriate action—which is not always a stopout.

Some stopouts, when pressed for a reason, say they're leaving school to work. But a number of follow-ups on what stopouts do while they're out have proven that earning money is rarely a primary goal. My own interviews suggest that just enough money is earned to support the real stopout goals.

The few researchers who have closely studied stopouts, among them Robert Cope, have concluded that money problems alone rarely push a student off campus; if he wants the degree, he'll find a way to get it. Loan, aid, and work-study programs have been proliferating to help students stay in school; if a student doesn't know about them, he ought to find out. Lack of funds should *never* be the cause of a stopout.

No stopout decision can be made wisely, unless the real reasons are understood clearly by the student. If you're considering a stopout, first investigate carefully your reasons, and the alternatives they suggest.

3

Timing the Stopout

JUST as eating against one's will is injurious to health, so study without a liking for it spoils the memory, and it retains nothing it takes in.

—LEONARDO DA VINCI

Ideally, you ought to stop out whenever it will accomplish more for you than staying in. Realistically, there are limitations on your alternatives. Almost every college likes its students to spend the entire senior year on campus, preferably without a break, and many schools won't accept your transfer after the beginning of your junior year.

A recent study that explores the timing of the stopout is Larry Yartz's 1974 research at Allegheny College. Its results suggest that the longer you stay at one school before stopping out, the more likely you are to return to that school when you stop in again. This is partially due to the sobering fact that the later you stop out, the more credits you'll lose if you stop back into a different college.

Another reason for stopping out earlier in your college career rather than later is that once you're well into your major, it's not advisable to interrupt an academic sequence for any length of time. Information vital to each subsequent course may be forgotten, so you will need extensive review to catch up with your classmates. This is especially true for science or math majors, whose courses build directly on previous courses in the sequence. The unfortunate paradox is that students who want to stop out solely for enrichment or for testing whether they can hold their own in the real world are more likely to think of a stopout only when they're into advanced courses.

Due to the large number of community-college students who transfer after two years, the end of sophomore year is one generally acceptable point to stop out. In four-year schools, this has always been a traditional stopout time—far more sophomores slumped in interest and performance and then dropped out, than any other level. Lately, however, freshman dropout statistics have been gaining on sophomore figures. And, interestingly, among the college dropouts studied by Robert Cope and William Hannah, one out of every four had already considered stopping out before he started college. These two newer trends are fast becoming popular.

Stopping Out Before You Start

More and more, high school guidance counselors are encountering seniors who are not interested in going directly into college. Many want to work or travel first while they get a better picture of who they are and what they want in a college. Many need a year to "find themselves."

Jon Mendelson grew up in a middle-class professional home in Maryland. His parents had been through college by dint of their own parents' struggles, and their degrees had given them careers and status. College was an automatic assumption in Jon's life.

But that changed in Jon's senior year. "I watched the other kids in my graduating class accept college without question, but I couldn't just go on without knowing *why* I was going. So I spoke to people who hadn't gone right on, and they were glad they hadn't." He decided to stop out.

Jon's decision shook the household. His father expressed fears about his "losing a year," his mother about his "hanging around doing nothing." They threatened to stop supporting him, so Jon looked for a compromise. "My parents said they'd accept my dropping out if I had a concrete plan of how I'd spend the year. I resented it. But I agreed that if they were financing me they were entitled to a say." He mapped out a plan for studying music in Philadelphia. He studied, traveled, worked for two years—and when he finally found a goal, he entered college.

What did Jon gain? "For the first time in my life, I felt independent in every sense except the financial one. I learned how to cope, to be by myself, to face hostility and not wilt."

There are many who advocate stopping out between high school and college. Kingman Brewster, Jr., president of Yale, is one. "I see too many students pushed *into* college by self-generated or imposed ambition; too many pushed *through* college by vocational panic. I'd like to see them take time out before they get here to broaden their sights, to break the continuity of academic pressures." The Carnegie Commission also would like colleges to permit students the option to "be admitted . . . but to defer entrance"—and urges parents to "assist by not pressing too hard for attendance of their children in college right after high school."

Stopping Out After a Year

There are good reasons for stopping out after the first year, just as there are advantages to stopping out before college. Having experienced college, a student may make better use of his time out, and wiser choices of school and program when he stops back in again. "After the freshman year," Dean Elizabeth Thomas of Pierson College at Yale told me, "the student is ready to take full advantage of the completely different opportunities for growth which exist off-campus." And Alexander Mood advises that once the student has "a very good grasp of what kinds of learning he can expect in institutions of higher education, he can then move into the world and begin to make his own assessment of the value of returning for more of that kind of formal education."

What Students Say About Timing The Stopout

The best time to stop out would probably be after the first year, when you've had a little taste of college. Go live a little bit, learn a bit more about yourself, come back with a little more direction . . . and then stop again before you go on to graduate school.

—LEIGH MC CULLOUGH

Some people may be better off maturing as individuals in school rather than somewhere else. But I've stopped out three times and I feel any time you make an objective decision that you're better off than being out of school than in school, you should stop out for a while.

—RICHARD REED

I was glad I went right on to college. I needed to get away from home and at college I was exposed to so many things: friends on heavy drugs, difficult situations to handle. The whole college experience helped me function better outside. To take time off, you need a certain amount of maturity.

—ELIZABETH SCHWARTZ

I would not advise people to take time out if they'll feel insecure about being on their own. My mother had suggested I stop out between high school and college, but I didn't feel ready then. Looking back, I know my decision to wait until I felt I could handle it was a wise one. In addition, my year at college had changed my attitudes toward grades; I knew that when I returned it had to be to a school that wasn't strictly traditional. —ROBERT BALABAN

I never thought about it until I reached my last year of college, when I seriously considered taking some time out before law school. Because lots of my friends were going right on, and there was the parental pressure, I buckled under. Soon I regretted my decision and requested a leave of absence. They weren't too anxious to give it to me, but forty out of five hundred had already done it. Having finished my first year, I knew what I was coming back to— the heavy reading schedule, the demands in class. That part of it was helpful. —WILLIAM ROBBINS

How Long to Stop Out

Although the Newman Report suggested between one year and two as the ideal duration of a stopout, and the Carnegie Commission thought in terms of continual, lifelong stop-ins and stopouts, most experts think in terms of a year off. A three-semester stopout was at one time recommended, but recent data seems to verify that a one-year leave is best. People who leave for only one semester usually do so with a specific purpose in mind and often return still partially uncommitted to college. On the other hand, those who are gone for three semesters or more often feel a sense of estrangement when they return to the college scene.

Nancy Silver Lindsay's 1974 report on Harvard stopouts asked returning students to correlate their present attitudes toward school with their lengths of leave. She found that in general, the more decisions the student made himself about his stopout, the more he got from his experience. Students who had been away three or more terms were the ones who had been the most dissatisfied with college courses before they'd left, and the most likely to leave without specific plans. She also discovered that most single-semester leavers had seen their stopouts as cop-outs, and that one-year leavers were the least likely to have been in academic trouble. Students who were away a year took short-term jobs that insured time as well as money for nonwork interests, especially travel. And the longer the stopout, the more likely a student was to learn about a new field.

Students who'd been away longer than a year had returned with renewed interest in education, but they were often unprepared to resume a student life-style. Doing so meant going through a period of adjustment, which some students expressed as "culture shock." However, the longer they were away, the more often they returned with greater direction and commitment to a major and a specific future plan which led to better work habits and higher grades.

How Colleges Have Adapted to the Stopout

As we shall see throughout this book, when colleges recognize an educational trend, they alter their programs to incorporate it. Thus, faced with the fact of the college stopout, many schools greatly expanded the list of acceptable reasons for a leave of absence. When stopouts began to occur between high school and college, the deferred admission was utilized to legitimize them. And now that colleges have noticed that many high school students who are ready for college are wasting a year in twelfth-grade, the early admission is gaining acceptance at more and more colleges. In this chapter we'll explore early and deferred admissions. (Chapter 7 will deal in detail with the leave of absence.)

The Deferred Admission

The deferred admission is nothing more than a college-sanctioned stopout that is taken *before* the student starts college. Twenty-eight percent of the four-year colleges in our survey have official deferred admission policies. But even where no official policy exists, many schools will permit an accepted student to postpone entrance for a year without having to reapply. And among schools that do ask you to reapply, for many it's just a formality; if you've been accepted before, your reacceptance is almost automatic. The only general exceptions to this practice are the public colleges.

There are usually three points to consider, if you want to defer admission for a year:

1. You should be able to describe afterward what you've accomplished during the year and especially how you feel you've grown through your experiences.

2. Some schools may reject you if you've attended another college—even part-time—during the stopout. Others will not only accept you, but will also grant credit for those courses. They will also probably regard these grades as a more accurate indication of your ability than your high school grades. So think twice before taking a course in which you might earn less than a C.

3. Since financial aid allocations change from year to year, you may not automatically receive the same aid package that was originally offered.

To request a deferred admission, write to the admissions director after you receive your letter of acceptance. Be sure to include what you're planning to do with the time. Sometimes the school will agree to a six-month deferment or will extend your stopout, if your plans change for good reason. But a year's deferment is preferred by most schools. The college should then tell you how to confirm your attendance on your return. Follow their instructions to the letter or the school will assume you have changed your mind about attending and will give your place to someone else.

The advantage of the deferred admission is that

guarantee of a place waiting in college—possibly even in the college of your first choice. It will be reassuring to you and your parents.

Deferring a Transfer

When Robert Balaban stopped out of college after a year at Kenyon, he applied to a number of schools and, during his interviews, asked if he could delay his transfer admission if he decided to remain out of school an extra year. "I was thinking of going to New Zealand and Australia, and I figured it might take me more than the seven or eight months remaining before September."

Several schools said a deferred transfer was indeed possible; others assured him admission if he would resubmit his application after the stopout. Only one college refused to defer the admission.

This option is usually unadvertised and unofficial. It's existence is worth bearing in mind.

The Early Admission

If you're a high school student considering a stopout and would like to experience a year of college first, you ought to consider early admission. Early admission has been in existence since the fifties, for students who can complete their high school programs early. It is an alternative for those college-bound students who have taken accelerated high school courses and who find, by the time they reach twelfth grade, that senior English is the only required subject left. Sixty percent of the four-year colleges now have official early-entrance policies, and 20 percent more have no set policy but will accept eleventh-graders. Many schools limit early admissions to "exceptional students only," while others set higher entrance requirements for these candidates than for regular students. There are colleges, however, that are actively looking for early applicants, among them Johns Hopkins in Maryland, DePauw in Indiana, and Webster in Missouri. A rule of thumb: you are most likely to find early admission at the small private schools with the highest tuition fees, least likely at the large public colleges which have to mass-process their applicants.

Two warnings about early admission:

1. Don't confuse it with *early decision,* which means that the college will notify applicants promptly as to whether or not they're accepted.

2. Many colleges that offer early admission won't let you take advantage of it unless your high school will give you a diploma in your junior year. This presents problems because many high schools *won't.* So before you consider this option, investigate carefully not only the college's requirements but those of your own high school. Your school district's policy may simply reflect a lack of awareness of the colleges' requirements. If you begin early enough, you may be able to effect a change.

There are disadvantages to early admission—especially for students who are not socially mature. There's some evidence that although these younger students do just as well academically as regular students, three times as many transfer out of their first college. The implication here is that high school juniors choose their colleges too quickly or too early for sound decisions. Instead of early admission, you might want to consider taking Advanced Placement courses during your senior year in high school. The pace is less frantic, the classes generally smaller, the environment familiar, the cost infinitely cheaper than a year in college—and you can earn college credits by taking Advanced Placement tests (see Chapter 11 for details).

4

Will a Stopout Affect Your Future?

IN 1971, the federal government's Task Force on Higher Education (the Newman Commission) pressed for a change in admission policies to favor students who had had some experience outside school. Graduate schools, it suggested, ought to consider requiring a break in college attendance of one or two years as a condition of admission. "Experiences outside education," it recommended, "would strengthen . . . motivation and increase students' ability to choose 'relevant' courses of instruction. . . . Costs would be reduced—for students would be more effective learners, and colleges would be more effective centers of learning."

Apparently many schools have heeded the Newman Commission's recommendation that stopping out be looked on without disfavor. If your school is like most, you won't be penalized for your stopout—your grades, graduation honors, and recommendations for postgrad training or awards won't be affected in any way. This holds true even if you're a premed student; you can, by and large, stop into any school as long as you fit in all your necessary credits before graduation. It is worth noting that the student with a below-C average will generally find it easier to get into a second school *after* a stopout than *without* one, because admissions officers have noticed that a stopout tends to improve motivation.

However, once you're out of college that stopout may weigh heavily on your record, whether your next step is more schooling or a job in your field. And when you're one of 45,000 applicants competing for 14,800 medical school places,* one of 121,200 Law School Aptitude Test candidates after the 37,000 law school openings,** or one of the hundreds of thousands of unemployed postgrads queuing up for a management job this year, you'll want to have it all going for you.

Graduate School

I'm applying to graduate schools this month, and I'm expecting my stopout and the switching I've done, from chemistry to architecture to psychology,

---

* Based on estimates for 1975–76 of the American Association of Medical Colleges.
** From American Bar Association. *Law Schools and Bar Admission Requirements: A Review of Legal Educaton in the U.S. Fall, 1973.*

*to be an incredible plus. The hopping around has
clarified my goals; I know precisely what I want to
do with clinical psychology. In addition, the jobs
I've held during my stopout—in psychiatric hospitals
and in work with disabled children—will convince
the admissions committees that I know what I'm
getting into.*

—LEIGH MCCULLOUGH

A stopout is not necessarily a blemish on your record
if you are pursuing an advanced degree in a field other
than medicine. In fact, if you've used your time wisely
—either to renew your motivation, solidify your goals,
or obtain experience in your proposed field—the stopout
may be, as Leigh McCullough anticipated, an "incredible
plus."

Richard Gummere, director of the Office of University
Placement and Career Services at Columbia University,
has noted that the mean age of applicants accepted to
Harvard School of Business has risen to twenty-five.
Law schools, too, he says, are looking for older people
who have experienced "real life." "The dean of Georgetown Law School told me that their ideal applicant
is twenty-seven years old, married, and has outgrown
some other career goal—and that he makes a very good
lawyer. However, it's my impression—although not based
on anything more than hunch—that *medical* schools will
penalize an applicant for doing something 'different.'"

Dena Rakoff, who is with the Harvard Career and
Placement Service, agreed. "The law schools like to see
applicants who've done other things besides just schooling,

but we're not sure about the medical schools." A premed study is now under way at Harvard to provide some answers to that question.

Since there was no completed survey on the policies of law and medical schools, I wrote to 28 medical schools (of 95 listed) and 19 law schools (of 33 which issue both LL.D. and J.D. degrees) at varying levels of selectivity. Four specific questions were asked:

1. When someone applies to your school, will the fact that he dropped out* of school for a while in any way affect his application?

2. Is it better for an applicant to have dropped back into the college he originally left, rather than another one?

3. Is a leave of absence considered more respectable to your admissions committee than a dropout or transfer?

4. Is a dropout between high school and college taken more lightly by you than a dropout halfway through college?

Before examining the replies, it's worth noting that whereas 63 percent (12 out of 19) of the law schools responded, only 32 percent (9 out of 28) of the medical schools did. It would seem safe to conclude that the law school admissions personnel are more relaxed about the subject of stopping out.

Medical Schools

Responses came from Mount Sinai School of Medicine, the Medical College of Pennsylvania, New York Medical

---

* In most of my inquiries I used the word *dropout* because *stopout* was a term with which very few people were familiar.

College, Harvard Medical School, Downstate Medical Center of the State University of New York, University of Alabama School of Medicine, Medical College of Georgia, University of Texas Medical Branch, and the University of Arkansas School of Medicine. Based on those replies, an applicant's best course seems to be:

1. To take his stopout before college (unless he's sure of getting into Harvard Med, which feels that any "constructive time out may make an applicant more rather than less attractive to us").

2. Failing that, to make certain that he has had good reasons for his stopout, that he's taken only one, and that he's used the time "constructively"—a word which may be defined differently by different schools.

3. To show that he returned after his stopout to a more demanding college than the one he left (or at least to the same school).

Excerpts from the replies follow:

> *It seems to me that the most important question would be the reason for withdrawing. Reasons which were clearly positive, or necessary (health, financial), would probably not have a detrimental effect. . . . Direct transfer to a superior school would probably be an asset. A relatively short period of time between high school and college would also have no consequence.*
>
> —MARIO A. INCHIOSA, JR., PH.D.,
> Co-Chairman, Admissions Committee,
> New York Medical College

> *The time out is well spent if it leads to self-understanding, if it is used to help others, or if it is spent*

in a health care related project. Our evaluation of "constructiveness" is made in relation to the partic- ular needs and qualities of the individual. For some students, time out may be a far richer educational experience than following conventional and some- times unimaginative career lines.

—LEON EISENBERG, M.D., CHAIRMAN,
Admissions Committee, Harvard
Medical School

. . . our application contains a question concern- ing whether the applicant's education has been con- tinuous, and the applicant should be prepared to explain any gaps. We might question an applicant's maturity and motivation if he drops out of college, but it would not really become an issue unless his academic record is below 3.50.

—JEROME P. PARNELL, PH.D., CHAIRMAN,
Admissions Committee, Downstate
Medical Center of the State
University of New York

In addition to the survey, I spoke to a number of doctors who serve on admissions committees for several well-known schools of medicine. With my assurances that their statements would be off the record, they all reported that they would tend to recommend rejection of ap- plicants who had taken stopouts. Since medical school requires arduous work and dedicated study, they felt students needing time off in college might not be able to make it through med school. One doctor summed it up: "I'd prefer to give the spot to someone who shows the drive to make it all the way through. As things stand, we have to turn away too many of them."

If you're just starting college and are interested in pre-med, you might investigate the new six-year college-and-medical-school combination programs at such places as Boston University and Northwestern. Because these programs are integrated under one aegis and their administrators are experimental in outlook, they may be receptive to a seven-year plan that includes a year's stopout. Also keep in mind that a number of dental schools still require only two years of college preparation for admittance. Another consideration: perhaps what you need is not a stopout, but the challenge of professional school.

Law Schools

The law schools that responded to my survey letter are those of New York University, Harvard, University of Pennsylvania, George Washington University, Tulane, Marshall-Wythe School of Law at the College of William and Mary, Temple, Georgetown, University of Illinois, University of Michigan, University of Texas, and Suffolk University.

Unlike their medical school counterparts, law school deans and admissions directors generally felt that stopping out would have very little bearing on admission. Attending more than one undergraduate school was also an acceptable—and common—practice among law applicants, although some law schools indicated that they preferred candidates who hadn't transferred to a less demanding college. The most important criteria for admission are grades and Law School Aptitude Test scores. The grade point averages before and after the stopout are usually compared to make sure grades went up, not down.

Daniel S. Kimball, the director of admissions at the New York University School of Law, wrote: "If there is no apparent positive motivation or effect of the interruption, the applicant may be at a disadvantage. On the other hand, if the time spent has been well-used and the level of academic performance improved, the applicant may have improved his chances for admission." Mr. Kimball cited travel or work for a year or two as positive use of the time. "However, if the break were after a mediocre freshman year, contained no additional work experience or projects, and resulted in no change in academic performance, the impression left would probably be unfavorable."

As a matter of fact, Robert G. Brown, the assistant dean at the University of Illinois College of Law, wrote that his school has recently adopted a deferred admission policy which permits accepted students to defer their enrollment provided they offer a logical reason. "These reasons, thus far, appear to be mainly financial," he said, "although I suspect that many are undecided as to whether or not they wish to pursue a legal education. We feel that this policy will result in a more motivated class, and, thus far, it has worked quite well."

If you're headed for law school, consider making early application in your junior year. There are law schools that will accept three years of undergraduate work as prerequisite for admission, i.e. you will not need a baccalaureate degree. If you apply to any of these schools and get accepted, you may be able to arrange a stopout after your junior year and still be assured of a place in law school.

The Business World

Most college graduates head out into the business world rather than for more schooling. How will a stopout affect their chances in the job market?

The Carnegie Commission suggests some cause for concern. "Employment offices," it reports, "minimize personal risks by making reference to prior certification rather than relying on their own judgment." The commission found that employers want evidence not only of skills, but of ability to accept training and discipline. With twice as many qualified applicants as job openings, perhaps personnel directors consider ex-stopouts less disciplined, and therefore less desirable.

To find out how stopouts affect future employment, I first posed the question in my 101-college survey. Fully 40 percent replied that they simply didn't know how stopping out affects job placement. Contrary to student assumption, course and career advice received at college deals very little with the postgraduate future. If a decision you make while still in school might adversely affect your future career, your advisers may not be aware of it to warn you. My survey indicates that many schools feel their obligations end when the student departs.

However, half the surveyed colleges had reached some conclusions about the employability of ex-stopouts. One-third felt that a stopout has *no* effect on future employment, and another 15 percent believed that if the stopout was well spent, or motivating, it could actually be an asset in the job application and interview. They suggest that you acquire good references during the stopout and avoid making the time off seem like a lark or a vacation. According to some schools, employers may look closely at the student's record after his stopout and compare it to his earlier grades, much the way some graduate schools do.

Several schools felt that although one stopout doesn't seem to matter to employers, a record of several stopouts makes businessmen leery. Of course, many schools said, it depends on the employer. But they felt that employers are beginning to understand and accept wide variations in educational patterns.

Charles DeCarlo, who was in IBM management for many years before he became Sarah Lawrence's president, understands both worlds. He feels that a subtle revolution is taking place within the white-collar community. First of all, he suggests, the new managers are young, relatively flexible, and open-minded and even large organizations are more receptive to new ideas than they were twenty-five years ago. Secondly, there's a scarcity of able people, and a well-rounded applicant is an attractive candidate. Most important, DeCarlo feels, when a person is really outstanding he can start anywhere in a company and soon be promoted to where he ought to be.

But even entry-level positions are hard to get these days. In a tight job market, employers can offer less money, ask for specific skills, and refuse to compromise. The people with the worst job prospects are untrained recent college graduates. Considering the competition, will a stopout be an advantage or a drawback to the job-seeker? I took the question to the employers directly*: "How do you feel toward applicants who have just graduated from college but who have taken out a year or more along the way?"

A number of general guidelines emerged:

1. If you're trying for a job with a small or medium-sized company—where you will be interviewed by the person you'll be working with—being a few years older and having seen something of the world will count more in your favor than against you, as long as you seem to have outgrown your wanderlust.

2. If your application will be sifted through a personnel office, and your resume shows unaccounted-for time lapses during college, it will be put at the bottom of the pile. To circumvent this, use a functional resume (see Chapter 8) and be prepared to explain your stop-out. Needless to say, if it was spent rebelling against the system, you've just lost the job; if it was used to widen your horizons, learn new skills, improve your

---

* Interviewed were five owners of small businesses of under twenty-five employees, four owners of middle-sized companies with personnel departments, college recruiters with American Can Company, Mobil Oil, Allied Chemical, and Chase Manhattan Bank, personnel directors at Dow Jones and Dow Chemical, and three owners of professional-job personnel agencies.

motivation, or even to make money, you won't have to worry.

3. For any job area such as sales, where you have to visit clients, maturity is a definite plus. But if you're going to be working with people your age who have worked longer and are earning more, you may not be hired. The employer knows from experience that after you are there a few years you will start feeling underpaid.

4. If you want to join a very large corporation, get in touch with its college recruiter. These people, who are used to dealing with stopouts, are adept at sizing up the total you. What do they look for? A background that shows decision-making abilities, maturity, and a capacity to pinpoint the position desired. Recruiters' pet peeve: "We get more liberal arts grads who say, 'I'm an English major. I can do anything.' Or, 'I'm an economics major and I'm willing to learn.' Will you tell students that we have no jobs for generalists?" How do recruiters feel about stopouts? Open-minded. "We recently hired a young man who'd dropped out of Hobart because he wasn't doing well, studied at a little college in Florida, and then went back to Hobart. When he came to us he knew what he wanted to do and had definite ideas about what he could contribute to our program."

The Three-Year Degree

Most personnel people process so many applications that they learn to take shortcuts. If the applicant is straight from college, a fairly common shortcut is to glance immediately at his age. If the age matches the year of graduation, they don't look for unexplained gaps.

One way to take a stopout and still graduate at the "normal" age is to take advantage of the new programs that permit you to earn a degree in three years. The Carnegie Commission has strongly supported three-year degree programs as means "to reduce the duplication of work between high school and college, to allow time for stopouts, to permit earlier entrance into graduate programs, and, generally, to save the time of students."

In some colleges, the programs involve three years of round-the-calendar attendance. In others, the credit requirement is lowered to eliminate the need for summer-session attendance. These shortened programs all pare down introductory-level courses, which are usually little more than reviews of high school material. Besides saving time, a few of these degree programs reduce college costs by one quarter.

There are disadvantages to consider, though. Students in the year-round three-year programs tend to have tight, tough schedules with few breaks. In some programs you're forced to choose your major early—especially if you're planning on science or math. In addition, few three-year colleges have much in the way of sports programs, publications, or student government. This can make it difficult to meet people and to form a group of friends.

A list of colleges that are offering three-year degree programs is included in the American Association of State Colleges and Universities' book *Restructuring the Bac-*

calaureate: *A Focus on Time-Shortened Degree Programs,* by Robert M. Bersi (available from the ASCU for $4.50 by writing to them at Suite 700, One DuPont Circle, Washington, D.C. 20036).

5

Is Stopping Out for Everyone?

TAKING time off is not for everybody. For people who know what they want to do, who don't question their goals or their motives, or who are too immature to use their time out wisely, stopping out may just be copping out.

—A FORMER STOPOUT

To be sure, stopping out is not always recommended (although such respected educators as Alexander Mood and Charles DeCarlo feel that every student can gain a great deal from the experience). Some students are perfectly content to go from high school to college, and right through college in four straight years. In addition, there are students who stop out because of needs that can best be fulfilled in another way. For example, financial problems, or a need for a different academic environment, do not necessarily call for a stopout.

There are distinct advantages to staying in college. Social and extracurricular activities are more abundant for the student. And while the close friendships that are formed through four years of living together can last a lifetime, stopouts often break up those half-formed relationships, sometimes irreparably.

Times of economic stress also have an effect on stopout considerations. When money is tight and work scarce, strangers are less generous, travel bargains harder to find, and job openings extremely limited. And during a depression federal monies are pumped into support programs to keep people from leaving school to compete in the overcrowded job market. When that happens, it may be more advantageous to stay in school than to stop out.

Circumventing Financial Problems to Avoid Leaving School

If you're thinking of stopping out solely because you think you can't manage school financially, do some careful double-checking before you make the move. With all kinds of grants, loans, and work-study programs sponsored by federal, state, and college agencies, lack of money for education is no longer sufficient reason to consider a stopout. Look into the following sources of funds.

Federal Programs

Grants

Basic Educational Opportunity Grant. This will pay a varying amount toward four years of college, junior college, or vocational, technical, or nursing school if you go full-time. The amount, based on need, varies from year to year. In 1974 payments of up to $1,400 were made, and if your parents owned no property and earned under $10,000 you were probably eligible. Write to Box 84, Washington, D.C. 20044 for information on eligibility.

The grant generally is not available to ex-stopouts unless their time out has been between high school and college, but schools are permitted to review individual requests on a case-by-case basis within the guidelines of the Department of Health, Education and Welfare.

Supplemental Educational Opportunity Grant. You can get this even if you're a half-time student, but you must be among the neediest in the country to qualify. It pays between $200 and $1,500 a year for a four- or five-year course of undergraduate study, not to exceed $4,000 for four years or $5,000 for five years. Your college has to agree to match the government's award for you to be eligible. Applications are only available through the financial aid officer at the school to which you're applying.

Loans

Guaranteed Student Loan Program. Federal law states that no student can be denied one of these loans for college, vocational or technical school, trade or business school, or even independent study. You need neither a high school diploma nor a statement of need as long as you're studying at least half-time. However, it's a direct transaction between you and your bank or credit union, even though the government insures the loan and will pick up some of the interest charges if your school attests to your need for the money.

You can borrow up to $7,500 for undergraduate or vocational study (a maximum of $2,500 a year) and up to $10,000 including graduate school, at a guaranteed interest rate of 7 percent. (Even if the government feels you don't *need* the money, and therefore won't pay the interest, you can't be refused this loan so long as it's for your education.)

There are specific conditions for repayment of this loan. You must spread repayment over a five-year period; that is, you cannot pay back in one lump sum. There is a ten-year limit to the debt, or thirteen years if you have spent some of that time in the Peace Corps or VISTA. And you must repay at least $360 per year, or more, depending on the amount borrowed. You're expected to begin paying off the principal between nine and twelve months after you leave school; this applies to stopping out as well as graduation. But you can discontinue payments if you go back to school.

Applications are available through schools, banks, or loan agencies, or inquire with your state department of education.

National Direct Student Loan Program. These are for undergraduate or postgraduate students, attending school at least half-time, who can show need for financial assistance.

Repayment begins nine months after you graduate; stopouts are given a nine- to twelve-month grace period before they must start repayment. If you use up your nine- to twelve-month grace period during a stopout, you will not have it available after graduation. Instead, you will be expected to start payment within thirty days, although a recent proposal suggested extension to sixty days. There are loan-payment deferral provisions for VISTA and Peace Corps volunteers, as well as total cancellation of the debt for special teaching or health service. For the loan or any renewal, see the financial aid officer at the school to which you're applying; after a stopout you may be asked to fill out a new financial statement.

To renew the loan after a stopout of more than a year, you must attend school full-time.

State Programs

The following states have educational *gift* programs (i.e., financial assistance that need not be repaid), for state residents only: Alaska, California, Connecticut, Florida, Georgia, Illinois, Indiana, Iowa, Kansas, Maine, Maryland, Massachusetts, Michigan, Minnesota, Missouri, New Jersey, New York, North Carolina, North Dakota, Ohio, Oregon, Pennsylvania, Rhode Island, South Carolina, Tennessee, Texas, Vermont, Washington, West Virginia, and Wisconsin. Stipulations and conditions vary with the state: some programs are restricted to use at colleges within that state, and some are only for low-income families.

The following states support their own loan programs,

which supplement the federally administered loans: Alabama, Alaska, California, Connecticut, Delaware, District of Columbia, Florida, Georgia, Idaho, Illinois, Indiana, Iowa, Kansas, Kentucky, Louisiana, Maryland, Massachusetts, Michigan, Minnesota, New Jersey, New York, Ohio, Pennsylvania, Puerto Rico, Rhode Island, Utah, Vermont, Washington, West Virginia, and Wisconsin.

Federal judges have recently ruled that women married to out-of-state residents are still residents of their own states for purposes of college application. But registering to vote in the state where you attend school will not automatically qualify you for state-resident tuition levels, grants, or loans.

Your state legislators or courts may have made additional educational provision for you. For example, in New Jersey you can even collect welfare and still go to school if you can show you're fulfilling vocational objectives by being there.

For fuller information about your state's offerings and provisions, write to your state's Commissioner of Education.

College Programs

Colleges have always had scholarship money set aside for needy students and "incentive awards" to attract top scholars to their campuses. The scholarship programs multiplied at immense speed during the sixties; recently incentive awards have proliferated.

Loan and award programs vary greatly from school
to school. For example, Yale and Duke have student loan
programs in which the borrowed money is returned at
a large interest rate, as a percentage of postgraduate
income earned over a thirty-five-year repayment period.
Many colleges, especially the most expensive ones,
have new loan programs aimed at helping the middle-
income student whose parents can't afford $6,000 or more
a year. They have also expanded those scholarship programs based on merit rather than need.

For complete information about what might be available to you, query the financial aid officer at each school
you're considering applying to. If you're already in school,
it's not too late to qualify for some of that aid money.

Community Agencies, Foundations, Corporations, Unions, Religious Organizations, Local Clubs, and Civic and Cultural Groups

Privately sponsored awards or loans may be available to
you. For example, the Women's Club of Great Neck, New
York, offers an $800 interest-free loan to anyone who
feels he needs it, and he doesn't have to prove financial
hardship. But because their policy is to avoid disclosure
of recipients of the loan, very few people in that town
know about its availability. A counselor at your local
high school will know what's being offered in your town.
For a list of good reference works that list privately
sponsored scholarships and loans, see the "Financial Aid"
heading in the Appendix.

Working Your Way Through

The federal government provides colleges with money to support jobs for students under the College Work-Study Program. This is not to be confused with college-sponsored work-study or "cooperative education" programs, which offer credit or salaries or both (see Chapter 9). You are eligible for the federally sponsored program if you are enrolled at least half-time as a graduate, undergraduate, or vocational student. Apply through your school's financial aid officer.

The program limits work to no more than forty hours a week, whether for the college or for an off-campus, nonprofit agency. Usually though, schools only permit up to fifteen hours of work a week, and will provide further financial assistance with grants or loans.

You'll earn at least federal minimum wage, but you'll have little choice about your job. So you may prefer to take your chances with your campus placement office, where you don't have to take the first job you're offered.

Under legislation enacted in June 1974, a private employer may hire up to four full-time students at 85 percent of the legal minimum wage (75 percent if he's involved with the student's school in a learn-by-doing project) if he first files application with the Labor Department. So if you need a job and know a place you'd like to work, it could pay to make an appointment with the boss and remind him about the new law. He might just find a spot for you with his company.*

* For further information, see the *New York Times*, June 18, 1974, page 39, column 2.

If you can't find a job, you can sometimes invent one. For ideas, see the books listed in the Appendix under "Job Exploration."

QUESTION: "Will holding down a job lead me to quit school?"

ANSWER: Believe it or not, it generally works the other way. Academic advisers report that students who hold jobs seem to make better use of their time and to buckle down more in their studies than students who do not have those responsibilities. Dr. Alexander Astin has found that as long as students work less than twenty hours a week, an on-campus job seems to increase their motivation for completing college.

QUESTION: "Can I avoid involving my parents when I request financial aid?"

ANSWER: A new possibility has been added to federal, state, and college financial aid programs by the proliferation of "emancipated minors" and "self-sustaining students." Both mean approximately the same thing—a college student who can show that for at least one year he has (a) lived with his parents no more than two weeks, (b) has not been claimed as a deduction on their income tax, and (c) has taken from them no more than $600 worth of money, gifts, food, clothes, medical care, and so forth. If he can verify the above three points, his father can be a millionaire and he may still qualify for student aid on the basis of *his* earnings and assets alone. This is not true at all schools, though. Some colleges—Yale, for example—will consider *no* student independent when he applies for admission, no matter what his parents' tax returns show. So the option requires checking with your own school.

QUESTION: "Will all this indebtedness interfere with my studying and my grades?"

ANSWER: No. As a matter of fact, the College Entrance Examination Board, which studied the effects of borrowing money for one's education, came up with these conclusions:

1. Undergraduate borrowing has little effect on whether a person goes on to graduate school or professional study —except in some cases to encourage it. Ex-borrowers stay longer in graduate school than nonborrowers, too.

2. People who have borrowed to finance college feel it has not influenced their decisions about marriage or their career choices. None had any regrets afterward about taking a loan.

When Changing Schools
May Be Your Answer

If being in the wrong school is the problem, weigh the alternative of transferring before you decide upon a stopout. Colleges vary a great deal in philosophical and social outlook, and there are strong academic differences to consider as well. It is not at all uncommon for a junior-college student to find after a year that he would prefer the challenge and variety of a four-year institution. And the student who must work hard for a C average at his four-year school will often relax and earn Bs at a lower-pressure, slower-paced two-year school. Other appropriate reasons for transferring: changing your major to one your present school does not offer, or being asked to choose a major before you're ready to decide.

Until the seventies, transferring was considered somewhat disreputable. (Nonetheless, in 1967 the Newman Commission discovered that in one major state college system, 30 percent of the seniors had attended three colleges and 17 percent had been in four or more.) When the two-year community college was developed, its students were expected eventually to transfer to a four-year school. Community colleges have been so enormously successful in accommodating the overflow of lower classmen from four-year schools, that at some universities more students are now transferring *to* community colleges than are being received *from* them.

In 1969, staff members of the College Entrance Examination Board studied the transfer policies of 146 schools. Although slightly dated, these are the only universal guidelines on the pitfalls and surprises awaiting transferees:

1. Most students don't know until *after* they've transferred how many of their credits will *not* be accepted by the new school. (In this study, 13 percent of the transferees lost a full semester's credit.)

2. Transferees from two-year colleges are slightly more likely to receive full credit than transferring four-year college students.

3. People transferring to small schools are twice as likely to lose a full semester as transferees to large colleges.

4. Transfer applicants have about the same probability

of being accepted by the college of their choice as do freshman applicants.

5. The only section of the country in which it is difficult to transfer is the northeast—and there, public colleges are harder to transfer into than private schools.

6. Although junior-college students who take occupational training programs have trouble transferring to four-year colleges, general program students in two-year schools are more likely to be accepted than persons who had the same grades in four-year schools! *

7. Fewer than one college in five has financial aid specifically earmarked for transfers. (Although a third of all freshmen at the surveyed schools received aid, only 11 percent of the transfers did.)

8. Colleges that require not-fully-refundable deposits of $50 or more within two weeks of notification of acceptance also seem to be those colleges which are not anxious to accept transfer students.

9. For students who want to transfer, the chances of being accepted may improve if you apply for a term other than fall, i.e., spring or summer, so don't assume you must matriculate in September. Many public colleges accept students in the summer; small schools often welcome spring applicants. (But check with the school; in some, spring admission is *more* competitive.)

A 1972 Massachusetts study indicated that because transfer applicants knew little about how to move to a new school, and got little help from the colleges to which

---

* Warning: good science departments in four-year colleges often award only half-credit, if that, for what they feel to be inferior teaching and inadequate lab experience at many two-year schools.

they moved, they were still losing out on credits and financial aid. More important, they were receiving no orientation or counseling. According to Richard D. Rooney, an associate director at the College Entrance Examination Board, "Transfer applicants generally received second-class treatment when compared with people applying as freshmen." Women transferees, this study found, travel third class: on the whole they need higher averages for acceptance than men, even though just as many females as males transfer.

In 1973, as a result of the study, a number of guidelines * were drafted to insure equal treatment for transfer students and these guidelines were distributed to every college in the country. The hope was that eventually transferees would cease to be second-class citizens; but on most campuses it's still more a future promise than a present reality.

If you can't choose between educational goals and a yen to travel, you can combine the two by transferring to a college at the other end of the continent or to an American, or at least English-speaking school overseas. Within the United States, there are colleges in Hawaii, Guam, Alaska, and Puerto Rico that welcome students from the mainland. Abroad, consider American College in Jerusalem, Israel; American College in Paris, France; American College in Switzerland; Schiller College Europe in Germany; and the University of the Americas in Puebla, Mexico.

---

* *Guidelines for Articulation for Receiving Institutions* is available free from the Massachusetts State Transfer Articulation Committee, P.O. Box 92, North Easton, Mass. 02356.

Before you sign papers or buy a plane ticket for any of these colleges, however, make certain that you totally understand the conditions under which you're being accepted by the school and that your credits can be transferred *back* should you plan to finish your education at home.

If you're in the wrong kind of social or academic milieu, a transfer may be all that's needed. But there are so many variations in ambiance from place to place, you may want to consider the alternative to a direct transfer: a short stopout in which you can investigate your choices. If you choose your second school in haste, you may find yourself even less comfortable in that college than in the first one.

Transfer students can keep some of their awards—for example, Merit and Westinghouse Science scholarships— by merely filing the correct papers. For full information, write to the donor of the award.

Traveling Without a Transfer

You may not need to stop out of school or even to transfer, if your main desire is to travel. Opportunity for travel is offered right within most colleges' academic programs, through summer and interim travel-study tours as well as semester and year-long study-abroad programs. You can study on the high seas with Chapman College's World Campus Afloat or Columbia University's Summer on a Schooner. You can do wildlife research in Tanzania, study nonviolence in India, or film tribal lore in

Guatemala. A 1972 survey came up with over five hundred semester or year-long study-abroad programs in the colleges and over three hundred travel-study programs.

An important aspect of many of these programs is that they're open to students from other schools. If you see an interesting study-abroad program in another college's catalog, check with your dean or adviser to see if your school will recognize it for credit. There are many fine books and pamphlets available that detail these hundreds of travel-study opportunities, some of which are listed under "Travel-Study" in the Appendix.

There are also a large number of commercial organizations that offer travel-study for the eighteen- to thirty-year age group. Many advertise in the pages of the *Saturday Review* and the *New York Times Sunday Magazine*. Try to avoid these. One reason is that travel-study with a college-sponsored tour will be much more likely to earn you credits for your money. Another reason: these independently sponsored tours are not all to be trusted. The Department of State, which receives the complaints of students stranded in other countries by some of the less reputable organizations, has published a free brochure called *A Word of Caution: Private Work, Study or Travel Abroad Organizations*. It suggests how to go about evaluating the group and its program before committing yourself to the tour. Read it before signing up with any private travel group. Write to: Director of Public Information and Reports Staff, Bureau of Educational and Cultural Affairs, Department of State, Washington, D.C. 20520. Despite company claims, there is *no* accreditation of private agencies by the regional college associations.

So check with your dean's office as to which private tours, if any, are accepted for credit.

Changing Your Major, or Living Without One

If your sole reason for stopping out is a fear that you've chosen the wrong major, or a resistance to your school's pressure on you to choose one, you do not necessarily have to stop out.

Colleges have begun to relax their insistence on early choice, largely because recent statistics have shown that the earlier a student is forced to choose a major, the more likely he is to stop out. Contributing to this policy change was a report by the Carnegie Commission that only one-third of graduates wind up in vocations related to their majors anyway. "The best education," a successful businessman told me, "is a general one which teaches you how to work and how to get along with people. Wherever you work, there'll most likely be a training program to teach you whatever facts you need to know."

If you're not ready to zero in on a major yet, ask your school if there's an alternative. While most colleges expect you to declare your major by the end of your sophomore or the beginning of your junior year, a number treat individual requests with flexibility. Many junior colleges and a growing number of four-year schools don't require a major at all. And some schools now permit you to design your own major.

A new option is becoming available: to defer your choice of major until you're certain of your career goals.

Colleges label this "unclassified," "undecided," "undeclared major," or "liberal studies." In some schools you may keep this status only until the end of your sophomore year, but in a few schools you can remain "undecided" until just before graduation. Not many colleges advertise or strongly encourage the "undecided" option. You'll have to seek it out with inquiries and special requests. The following is a partial list of schools that offer the option.

Anna Maria (Massachusetts)
Arkansas (Arkansas)
Bradley (Illinois)
Bucknell (Pennsylvania)
Fort Lewis (Colorado)
George Mason (Virginia)
Hampshire (Massachusetts)
Incarnate Word (Texas)
Iowa Wesleyan (Iowa)
Jacksonville (Florida)
Lindenwood (Missouri)
Mary Washington (Virginia)
Miami University (Ohio)
Millikin (Illinois)
Mount St. Mary (New York)
New Mexico Institute of Mining and Technology
    (New Mexico)
State University of New York at Buffalo (New York)
University of Pennsylvania (Pennsylvania)
Washington (Maryland)
Wittenberg (Ohio)

6

Planning and Financing the Stopout

HAVE a plan," stopouts urge those who follow in their footsteps. "Understand your reasons." "Articulate your goals." "Know what you want from your time."

If you don't have a plan, you're pretty certain to return to school—as several stopouts did—with the same unanswered questions that made you decide to leave. And before long you'll be thinking about stopping out again.

How to Decide What to Do

Judy Seaton was a biology student when she stopped out. Her needs were clear to her. "I wanted to get the feeling of what I would actually be doing after graduation, have a change from my urban, academic milieu, and pick up brownie points toward future veterinary school if I decide to take that route. So I investigated the chances of working on a farm upstate."

The first thing you'll have to do is to determine your own needs. List all the reasons why you're stopping out (Chapter 2 suggests the most popular reasons for stopouts). These reasons, taken together, should clearly indicate your stopout goals.

Then determine what activities will help you accomplish these goals. (Work of some kind? Travel? Learning a skill? Ask yourself if making money is important, or will you need just enough to support your other goals? Is living with a group important, or do you need to make your way alone?) List these activities in order of their importance in helping to accomplish your stated goals. Then rank them in order of personal preference. If there's any great discrepancy between the two lists, you may be on the wrong track, pursuing something you do not feel firmly committed to. Do some soul-searching; rethink your needs and goals.

The next step is to determine how long you will stop out, and to fit your planned activities into the allotted time span. This may involve some juggling. One suggestion is to overlap some activities. For example, part-time volunteer work can be woven in with guitar lessons; traveling on your own will test your ability to survive independently. But don't try to do too much, or you'll end up feeling unfulfilled no matter what you are involved in.

If Your Goals Are Unclear

Many students, when asked their reasons for stopping out, reply, "If I knew what I wanted, I'd be set. All I do know is that I *don't* want to stay in school." Students who don't understand *why* they want to stop out or *what* they hope to accomplish, may really be better off in college until their reasons are clearer.

On the other hand a general desire to experience life outside of school is a legitimate reason to stop out. College President Charles DeCarlo suggests, "Use the time to do something as new and different to your life as it can possibly be. Test yourself; at the same time you'll be testing your educational plans."

With so many options available, how does one choose the best ones for him? Some college career offices offer a minicourse called DIG (short for Deeper Investigation of Growth), which uses group and one-to-one counseling techniques. The DIG course, designed by Richard Gummere of Columbia University, is essentially a career development workshop which can help you decide where you're headed.

If your school doesn't offer DIG or its equivalent, you can do your own goal-planning with the help of the books listed under "Goals Exploration" in the Appendix.

Where to Find Help If You Need It

When I told my parents I wanted to stop out, they were furious, since they had chosen the school for me. They said if I quit this school they wouldn't pay for me anywhere. They stuck to their word.

—FREDERICK SELTZER

I assumed my parents would be upset, so first I told them I was thinking of transferring. When I finally got the nerve to say I was taking time off, I kept reassuring them that I would go back, and when they believed it, they became supportive.

—ELIZABETH SCHWARTZ

Many parents are like Elizabeth's, fearful that if you take time out to think about it you may decide school isn't that important to you. Some are like Frederick's, totally unresponsive to your views. Others are like John R. Coleman, president of Haverford, who wrote in *Blue Collar Journal,* "When my oldest daughter called to say she was taking a leave from Earlham College [I said,] 'Nancy, I didn't mean *you* when I advocated that students drop out.'" Yet, he admitted, "She proved to be right in taking that leave."

Your parents may overreact to your decision. They may feel they're losing influence over you, so they might be unduly negative about your plans. But if you make clear your need for their continuing guidance and encouragement, you can gain their support, if not their understanding. In their study of college stopouts and dropouts, Robert Cope and William Hannah found that of those who discussed the decision with their parents, 77 percent found them supportive. Very few parents were as unrelenting as Frederick's.

Older brothers and sisters are often as helpful as

parents. Since over 90 percent of college students think about leaving school before they graduate, an older sibling has probably investigated it before you.

In addition, at most colleges there are special school officials who deal with stopouts. You may not have heard of them—consult your student handbook, or ask around. Surveys reveal that *less than half* of all students bother to contact *any* adult who's in a position to help them with any obstacles in their collegiate development—although when they do talk to deans and professors, the majority are found to be helpful.

Robert Cope suggests that unless you do discuss bothersome program limitations with college personnel, you may never know whether there is room in your school for modification or flexibility. "Sometimes," he said, "a student may leave unnecessarily when the college would willingly make possible the curricular or extracurricular activities which he would like to pursue."

Another place to find help, especially if total objectivity is what you need, is with one of the educational-vocational counseling services that are available throughout the country. Although you must be wary in choosing a counseling service, since they are unlicensed and unregulated, you can be guided by the screening capabilities of the International Association of Counseling Services, the only recognized accrediting organization in America. Its *Directory of Counseling Services*, published every two years, is available for $4.00 by writing the International Association of Counseling Services, Inc., 1607 New Hampshire Avenue, N.W., Washington, D.C. 20009, or check your local library. The *Directory* lists the complete range of services provided by each accredited agency, and the fees for those services. Many of the listings are college counseling offices.

A Stopout Plan Follow-Through

I had two goals for my time off: first, to unwind from school's hectic pace; and second, to decide on a new major. I left school in June and spent the summer at my parents' house, working three days a week for my father, and enjoying my leisure time.

That summer, I evaluated all the things I'd done in school, what I'd enjoyed and what I'd been disappointed with. I realized that I'd gotten enormous satisfaction from a two-year Human Development course in my nursing major—especially working with retarded children and then at the Juvenile Aid Bureau. I'd seen a strong correlation between special education and juvenile delinquency, but my teacher didn't see how they could mesh. Now, out of school with time to think, I realized that his inability to see it didn't make it wrong, and that there might be other schools that would allow me to combine studies in the two fields.

I had accomplished both my original goals by September, so I set two new ones: first, to get experience in a juvenile court; the second, to find a school where I could take a special ed-delinquency major. Trying to get experience didn't work out! I could have done volunteer work in court, but no place would take me

*on for pay and I wasn't about to sponge off my
parents.*

*But I did find a school, so I cut short my stopout
and am starting there in January.*

—ELIZABETH SCHWARTZ

Shelter: *You Can't Go Home Again*

What Thomas Wolfe had in mind was not necessarily that
you'll find the doors locked, but that you will have ma-
tured while away, into a near stranger. "Living at home
for the [stopout] year," Charles DeCarlo said, "is disaster."
That may even be true if your stopout comes between
high school and college. Stopouts seem to know it intui-
tively: a prime stopout goal is to attempt real independence.

Some parents force the issue by declaring, "If you
quit school, don't count on us for support." You may avoid
a possible impasse with your parents by announcing right
away that you want to rely on your own resources during
your stopout.

Or, your parents may unwittingly sabotage your attempts to go it alone. They will cajole you home, fix up
your old room, prepare your favorite foods, plan fishing
trips, and prod their friends for jobs for you. (Unfortunately, they're still psychologically oriented to the theory
that you're not an adult until you're twenty-one, even
though legal maturity has been lowered to age eighteen
in most states.) So keep in mind those goals you've articu-
lated.

I would have done better if I had my own apartment. When I was at school I started my own way of life. When I came back I had to respect my parents' values—church, television serials, the whole bit. I was miserable and they were miserable even though we had been a close-knit family.

—MARY LOU TORNES

It wasn't my parents—they tried to let me do my own thing—but their friends and relatives. Every time they came to the house I'd hear, "Don't you know you're killing your parents?" and "If you were my kid I'd never've let you quit school." After a few months of that I had to get out. I should have done it in the first place.   —SALLY TIMKINS

You may have no choice but to live at home. It can work—but only if you follow two rules. First, pay in currency and/or services for your food-clothing-shelter. Second, insist on a room of your own.

If you're not living at home, then *where*? Leasing an apartment will present complications. Even if you found a place you could afford, a landlord who'd accept your signature, and a lease that ran less than two years, it would involve a commitment to remain in one place, which you may prefer to avoid. Consider instead apartment sharing with a roommate who has his own lease, or find a commune or co-op arrangement.

Advice from other stopouts: living with a roommate has all the pitfalls of college dorm living without any guarantee of the roommate's stability, financial or emotional. Before you move in, make sure you not only discuss ground rules, but that you are relatively sure of the stranger's maturity. (One way is to talk to his last roommate.)

Money

None of the students I interviewed had spent his entire stopout on his parents' dole. Each one felt it had been important to earn his way. For some, that meant refusing to borrow money; for others—usually those whose parents could afford the added expense—the line was drawn less rigidly.

There's nothing wrong with borrowing from parents, if you pay back. There's nothing wrong with using their Blue Shield if you're still covered under their policy, or the family's extra car if it's offered. But taking a cross-country trip on your parents' American Express card suggests a lack of independence on your part.

In planning your stopout, you've got to think about a budget. Yet it's the one thing many stopouts consider least, traveling until their money runs out, then wiring for a loan and grabbing a job to pay it back. This stopout's experience is by no means atypical:

> *I went to Wisconsin because I had a good friend there. I figured I'd find a place to live and a job, but I spent three weeks walking my feet off and I couldn't find either. So I went down to Nashville. No luck there either. After two weeks my money ran out and I wired for the fare home. Then it took me two months to find a job as a clerk, filing forms. I hate it—it's an idiot's job—but I feel I've got to pay my father back the money I borrowed.* —JOHN BERLE

With a little budget planning before he began his stopout, John would have used his time better. He needed not only a goals plan but also a money management plan. Here's how to make one. Enlist the help of someone who's been handling money more than you have—a parent or a friend who's been on his own at least six months. You'll need his advice in estimating your liabilities.)

Money Management Plan

ASSETS (*Funds Available at the Start*)	AMOUNT
Savings accounts	$
Checkbook balance	
Government bonds*	
Loans available*	
Stocks*	
Cash on hand	
TOTAL ASSETS	$

LIABILITIES (*Estimate of Stopout Expenses*)	*Per Week*	*Total Stopout*
Shelter	$	$
Clothing (include laundry)		
Food (include snacks)		
Transportation (gas, tolls, fares)		
Auto payments and insurance		
Medical and drugs		
Entertainment (include records, cigarettes, dates)		

* Include these reserves only if you're ready to draw on them for stopout support money.

Education (include books,
    music lessons)
Miscellaneous

TOTAL LIABILITIES	$	$
Subtract Assets		
NEEDED TO EARN	$	$

Now that you have a ball-park idea of how to apportion
your money during your stopout, follow it closely to keep
track of your budget. Halfway through your stopout (or
sooner if your balance begins to dip low), do another
money management plan; you can then adjust your
activities accordingly.

7

How
to
Leave
College

THIS chapter is for the more than 50 percent of college students who will, according to statistics, start their stopouts without making any preparations for coming back. (High School students: please see the paragraphs on deferred admission and early admission in Chapter 5.) If you fall into this group, you may be convinced at this moment that you never again want to see the inside of a campus gate. But you also may be one of the more than 85 percent who will discover, once you're out, that you do want to return.

Try to comply with your school's regulations when you leave. Making the move by the rules may take a little more time and effort, but you'll save time and possibly money when you return. In addition, your school may offer all sorts of services for stopouts which you'll never discover unless you notify them of your plans.

The Withdrawal

Most schools have two distinct categories for exiting students: the withdrawal, for people who are not expected back, and the leave of absence, for those who are.

You can withdraw for "academic" or "medical" or "personal" reasons. If you do it officially, and you're less than halfway into a semester when you do, you are probably entitled to rebates on the semester's tuition and meal tickets (but not for your dorm charges). So if you must withdraw, do it officially.

But the withdrawal should be used only if you can't qualify for a leave (in other words, if you absolutely must leave school in the middle of the term), or if your school is one of the few that doesn't offer leaves. In most colleges, if a student withdraws, his affiliation with that college ends. He can reapply at any time, but when he does his application will be competing with many others. Most likely, he will be put through the same rigid admission criteria as the school's regular transfer applicants.

There are, of course, exceptions to this general rule: some schools keep you on "interim" status indefinitely, and others readmit any former student who writes a letter of request.

Though the number of alternatives is increasing* the

* Alexander Astin writes, in *Preventing Students from Dropping Out,* ". . . some institutions are introducing administrative procedures to classify as stopouts those students who formerly would have been called dropouts, in order to simplify their reentry."

simplest method of leaving school is still completing your present term before withdrawing. If your record shows an unwillingness to finish what you start, you can expect to be questioned closely about your "seriousness of purpose" when you reapply anywhere.

The Leave of Absence

If your school offers leaves of absence, take advantage of the opportunity. Because if you withdraw, you're no longer a student, and no longer entitled to student discounts, rates, and other benefits. If you take a leave, technically you're still a student at your college; you may be entitled to continue its student insurance plan, to take courses at reduced rates, and, in some instances, to buy a meal ticket or rent a room on campus if it fits in with your plans.

In addition, if you take a leave of absence you will remain a member in good standing of the campus community. If your marks are adequate when you leave (and most students leave with a C average or better), you'll be welcomed back with no red tape and all your credibility intact, just as long as you followed the school's rules about taking a leave. Those rules usually include the following:

1. See the necessary people and sign the necessary papers by the school's request deadline. You can always withdraw the request, with *no* penalty whatsoever, if you change your mind before registration day. If in doubt about whom to see, the dean of students is a good choice.

While the deadline for a fall-term leave may be as early as April, there is some flexibility, because college staff recognize that students often decide on a fall leave during the summer. But the deadline for a spring leave, usually some date during the final two months of the fall term, is not as flexible.

2. Designate a specific term when you'll be back. School rules usually demand that you indicate on your leave of absence request form the date when you promise to return. Most schools limit you to a year, although here again there are many variations—including five-year and limitless leaves—so it's wise to check with your own school.

Do set a definite time for return; this has the intrinsic value of helping you plan your stopout. For the school, it's vital; if it knows when the stopouts are returning, it can better plan its transfer intake numbers.

3. Have a good reason for wanting a leave. A good reason today can be almost any reason that makes educational sense to you—even, as the Yale catalog states, "for an experience of a different sort" than schooling. You must be prepared to present to the proper persons a plan of what you intend to do, and to assure them that you are truly sincere about your education.

Some good reasons for a leave (from the Mount Holyoke bulletin): ". . . to work, to travel, to study at another institution of higher education, etc." (Etceteras are loopholes; used properly, they can signify almost anything.) Included in *personal* reasons can be a desire to clarify your education or life goals before going on. Among the *academic* reasons can be simply a desire to have a differ-

ent educational experience by studying independently, or
at a different kind of institution, or in some special
program. The Vanderbilt University leave-of-absence flyer
says that its administration will accept as a valid reason
the desire to "find oneself" or gain a sense of direction.

How to Extend or Shorten a Leave

A college usually won't hold you to your original return
date as long as you have a *good* reason for wanting either
to return sooner or extend your leave. So don't be afraid
to request a stop-in date change if you really need one.
Send a letter to the dean of admissions or other appropriate person stating when you're expected back, when you'd
prefer to come back, and the reasons for the change.

However, keep two things in mind:

1. Sometimes the school's willingness to take you back
at an unscheduled time depends not on class space but
dorm space. If you change your stop-in plans, make sure
to reserve a room far enough in advance.

2. Since financial aid money is often apportioned among
students on a yearly basis, if you're coming back in the
spring you may have to forgo aid for that term.

How to Reserve a Place for Yourself

Whether withdrawing or taking a leave of absence, there
are three bases you ought to touch:

1. *Your dean or adviser or counselor and/or the ad-*

ministrative assistant listed in the student handbook.
He will have the proper forms for you to sign, and will
be able to explain some of the advantages of a leave
over a withdrawal. (If he doesn't volunteer the information, don't hesitate to ask direct questions.)

In many schools there is a formal "exit interview" procedure. Take advantage of it to get all your questions
asked and your facts straightened out.

While you're in the dean's office, be sure to ask for a
letter on school stationery notifying "whom it may concern" that you're "a student in good standing on leave of
absence from name-of-college for the year or years as
follows." It's a must in order to obtain an International
Student Identity Card (see Chapter 8). A few schools also
give leave-of-absence ID cards. A card keeps better and
is easier to flash when you're on line for tickets or cashier-
window student discounts. (If you extend your leave, be
sure to request a new letter or card.)

2. *Your financial aid office or the office of the bursar.*
Here's where you'll find accurate data on which scholarships (of those paid by or through the school) you will
be permitted to reserve for use after your stopout. In
addition, be sure to ask whether you can defer some of
your aid money without losing it entirely.

Although many colleges pass on to others any unused
aid money, a number are willing to defer some of their
grants and awards for six months or a year—or at least
to guarantee you'll get the same aid package on your
return (assuming, of course, that your Parents' Confi-
dential Statement remains the same). Try to get it all in
writing. And think ahead! When you're stopping in again,

be sure to apply for aid renewal before the required deadline of the term before you restart school. College personnel have told me that a large number of students lose out on aid simply because they apply after the school's reserves are already apportioned.

Many of the state award and loan programs have leave-of-absence clauses, and some even permit transferring after your leave. Ask your financial aid officer or bursar for advice, and be sure to file whatever aid-deferral forms are required.

(For stopout information on federal aid and loan programs, see Chapter 5.)

3. *Your career and job placement office.* When a student takes a leave of absence from the University of Pennsylvania, the school offers to place him in an academically relevant job and then provides "pre-job preparation, in-field follow-up, and reentry preparation counseling." Many other colleges have job and school referral services for students leaving to work or, as is becoming more and more popular, to study someplace else.

Letters to Write

Most schools provide leave forms for filing in triplicate at the beginning of your "exit interview" or its equivalent. If none is provided, be sure to have a request letter placed in your official file. A letter is proof of your "seriousness of purpose" and your commitment to return to the school if things go as planned. The letter might read:

Dear Dean ———:

After serious consideration, I have decided it would be best to interrupt my education at ——— College for a year in order to clarify my educational goals. I plan to spend the year working either for pay or voluntarily in a political context, to take a correspondence or continuing-education course in stenography, and to travel to other parts of the United States if I can earn enough money to do so. If I am granted a leave, I plan to return to ——— for the fall term of ———, either committed to a political science program of study or motivated toward a major in some allied field.

Sincerely,
Leonard Goldfarb

Observe: Leonard has included (a) length of leave desired, (b) his reasons, (c) his plans and their relevance to his educational commitment, and (d) the expectation that he will return—although, as his college well knows, his plans may change later on.

In addition to the leave request, many schools require letters officially petitioning for deferrals of financial aid. Even if a written request is not required by the school, it is always good insurance to have one on record. It might read something like: "I am taking a one-year leave of absence beginning (date). I hope I may renew my current financial aid when I return to campus."

Letters should also be written to any off-campus organizations from which you may be receiving direct financial assistance that isn't funneled through the college. For example, Westinghouse Science Foundation scholarships can be retained, on notification, by students who stop out in good standing (although they cannot be deferred between high school and college).

How Many Times Can You Stop Out?

Of the 101 schools that replied to that question, only Yale reported a set policy which permitted no more than one readmission after withdrawal. The other schools asserted that they either have no policy or one that is responsive to individual circumstances.

Numerous schools said that they would readmit a student any number of times as long as he was in good standing, or as long as his reasons for stopping out remained credible. Others said they would seriously question the commitment of a student who took more than two stopouts. However, one prestigious school volunteered the case of a student who stopped out four times without penalty.

Some schools provide for periods spent off campus *within* their programs. For example, at the College of the Atlantic in Maine, registration is not required for every term. Once you matriculate, you're a member of their student body until you withdraw from the college. At Colgate University you can take up to eight months off without losing time toward your degree. Under the new Dartmouth Plan, effective since the fall of 1972, the usual four years of college are divided into nineteen terms and only eleven are required for graduation. They can be grouped in any sequence, or taken consecutively for a graduation after only three years. (Stopout semesters that are included as part of a college's curriculum, such as mid-year work-study plans, are discussed in Chapter 9.)

What Happens to Your Class Standing When You Stop Out?

Stopping out, no matter how frequently, has no influence on class standing or eligibility for awards and honors at graduation. These are determined by scholarship and academic performance alone, and there is no penalty for time gaps in your record.

(Admission to graduate and professional schools is, however, a separate consideration, as previously discussed in Chapter 6.)

What If You Want to Stop Out and Then Transfer to Another School?

Some stopouts just want a furlough from the school they left. (Harvard, for example, has a high stopout rate, yet most of these students return to graduate from Harvard.) But statistics suggest that a greater number stop into another college more in line with their areas of interest or their temperaments. They use part of the stopout time to investigate new campuses, and in some cases to enroll in a course or two.

One student, for example, left St. Johns University to find a school with a more lenient math requirement. With a friend from Reed College she sampled a term at the University of Wisconsin. It convinced her that St. Johns was, though demanding, the better school for her. Her friend, however, preferred Wisconsin to Reed, and decided to transfer.

Even if you plan never to return to your first school, take the leave of absence anyway, and retain your student status. When you've been accepted at another school, you can cancel your leave.

Don't hesitate to request transcripts for the schools you're applying to even when you're on official leave. Clerks and secretaries fill transcript requests automatically for all students—even those fully enrolled and attending classes—with no questions asked about intentions.

Can You Try a New School While on Leave?

Sampling a new college during a leave of absence has become so commonplace that many colleges have set up exchange plans enabling their students, *within their normal programs,* to take up to a year's worth of courses elsewhere for full credit. (This program, bulletins warn, is not intended as a preliminary to transferring. But, as studies at Wheaton have shown, this situation is often unavoidable.) Before you decide upon a leave, check whether your school has an exchange program with a college you might like to sample.

Some examples of exchange programs:

> **The Thousand-Mile Campus:** on-going exchanges among the nineteen California State campuses.

The New York Visiting Student Program: full exchange among sixty New York state colleges and universities, public and private—even including the revolutionary Empire State College.

The Twelve-College Exchange: Amherst, Bowdoin, Connecticut College, Dartmouth, Mount Holyoke, Smith, Trinity, Vassar, Wellesley, Wesleyan, Wheaton, and Williams.

The Five-College Program: Amherst, Hampshire, Mount Holyoke, Smith, and the University of Massachusetts.

The Four-College Cooperation: Bryn Mawr, Haverford, Swarthmore, and the University of Pennsylvania.

The Maryland Program: Goucher, Loyola, Johns Hopkins, Morgan State, Towson State, and the Maryland Institute College of Art.

The Nashville University Center: 5 colleges.

The Chicago Group: 8 colleges.

Individual arangements, such as the one between Williams and Howard.

Special multicampus colleges like University Without Walls and the expanding Antioch program.

In addition, the National Student Exchange, a new organization, places students for one term or more on campuses they consider markedly different from the student's own. So far, the Exchange has nineteen colleges participating. For information, write Richard L. Desmond, Dean of Faculties, Indiana University at Fort Wayne, Fort Wayne, Ind. 46805.

8

Working
and
Wandering

SOMEDAY we may find a broader recognition of the need for rhythm in young people's lives, the need for times of deep, disciplined involvement in formal study and then for times of paid work and travel of more than a summer's length.
—JOHN R. COLEMAN,
in *Blue-Collar Journal*

Work and travel are by far the most common stopout activities. There are a number of options in both categories, which merit careful consideration before you settle on one stopout plan.

Working

Stopout Paul Lazes told me, "My grandfather left me an educational fund, which paid out only while I was in school. So I economized and saved during my year at college. That enabled me to spend the time out of school doing what I really wanted—building a house on a piece of land I'd bought—without financial worries."

For most people, saving up beforehand isn't enough, and some paid work will be necessary to make ends meet during a stopout. But besides the survival factor, there are other good reasons for working:

1. *To explore options.* If you're clear about your goals, you've probably considered stopout activities that include learning more about various careers. If you're a science major, you may want to try a laboratory job; if you're a psych major you may want to work in a clinical setting. Taking a short-term job—even at the clerical or bottle-washing level—can familiarize you with your future surroundings should you want to stay with your major.

2. *To explore yourself.* If you're skeptical as to whether you can learn anything about yourself digging ditches or washing dishes, read John R. Coleman's *Blue-Collar Journal: A College President's Sabbatical.*

3. *To boost your future.* Even if you can't earn credits toward graduation (see Chapter 11, Credit for What You Already Know), the right job experience correctly presented on a resume or the right reference letter from an employer can help immeasurably in landing your first post-college job or getting into graduate school.

There are two basic categories of work: jobs that pay, and volunteer work, in which the real payoff is in experience or in helping a cause.

Working to Make Money

There are two approaches to working: you can either work for someone else or be your own boss. For the latter you need a skill or a craft. Your skill can be as basic as dealing well with children, your craft as common as photography. Everybody has *one* thing he can do superbly. You can work alone or form a co-op. (See "Job Exploration" in the Appendix.)

Although during the sixties craftsmen could usually count on a sale, it's not easy to sell crafts at a time when people are on tight budgets. So before you buy the ingredients for two dozen loaves of banana bread, make sure there's a market to sell them to. Even though health food, for instance, continues to be popular, many health-food stores folded in 1974 and 1975.

Changes in economic outlook also affect the way you must approach job hunting. When companies are cutting back on their staffs to save money, not only are there fewer jobs, but you're competing with experienced workers seeking permanent positions.

Job Hunting

Have you been to the placement office of the college you're leaving? A number of schools actively counsel their students, suggest leads, and in some cases set up interviews with potential employers. Beloit in Wisconsin, for example, offers even its deferred students job counseling. Other schools may belong to stopout-job clearing-houses—or, with enough pressure from students—may be induced to form one of their own.

The first clearinghouse was established in 1974 at Northeastern University. Called the College Venture Program, its purpose is to provide jobs—both paying and volunteer—for "those interested in a structured leave-taking from their campuses." The Venture personnel will try either to find a job relevant to the student's major career interests, or will provide him with a chance to explore a totally new field without having to commit himself to any future in it.

Venture so far includes seventeen colleges, and other schools are joining rapidly. It has already placed students with citizens' action groups, within business and industry, on political campaign staffs, and in overseas jobs. Some of the Venture member schools give academic credit for the experience. Request information from your school's placement office, or write to College Venture Program, Institute for Off-Campus Experience and Cooperative Education, 360 Huntington Avenue, Boston, Mass. 02115.

Venture will simplify job-hunting—but it may also deprive you of a worthwhile experience. Many educators who favor stopouts, such as President Charles DeCarlo of Sarah Lawrence, believe that lining up your own work options will help you learn to make independent decisions. Particularly if your stopout goals include exploration of your future alternatives, they suggest that you do your own job search.

The majority of stopouts begin in the summer. If yours will, you might want to use that time to make the money you'll live on later. In the Appendix, under "Job Exploration," are listed three publications that will specifically help you find a summer job.

Another way to work without having to make any long-term commitments is to register with a temporary work personnel agency in your area. Most employ you for a week at a time, but some pay at the end of each day. Check under "Employment Agencies" and "Employment Contractors—Temporary Help" in your yellow pages.

Five Tips for Stopout Job Hunters

1. The old-style resume is particularly ill-suited to people who haven't held many jobs. Instead, write a letter accompanied by a functional resume (see explanation later in this chapter). Try to sidestep personnel agencies and personnel offices: both are fairly rigid and less willing to make innovative hiring decisions. Go directly to the person at the top of the company you're applying to, or to the one who would be your immediate supervisor.

2. Try the technique of "interviewing for information." Successful people are pleased and flattered by such an approach. Write to the president of a firm you're interested in and request an interview seeking career information about the business. If he seems receptive, query him about openings within his company.

3. What do you say when your interviewer asks if

you will be returning to school? One college career adviser suggests, "Since the statistical chance of any one
student's going back after a year is about fifty-fifty, I
counsel my students, 'You're unfair to yourself and your
employer if you tell him you will return to school when
you just as well might not.' Undergraduates might point
out to their interviewers that they'll need more schooling
but that they would like the employer to help determine
when more education is needed and just what kind.
Alternatively, a student might want to say, 'Yes, after a
year I may find I need more education to advance in
this field. But I hope to keep working for you summers
and then come back here after I get my degree.'"

4. If you can use your parents' contacts to get you a
job interview, don't bypass the opportunity. Despite this
advantage, you can still lose the job by not being direct
and convincing during the interview. (Henry Kaiser once
agreed to interview a friend's son. "What can you do?"
he asked. "I can do anything," said the son. Kaiser
replied, "If you could attach paper clips or type letters
or draw straight lines, I might be able to find something
for you. But I haven't got an 'anything' department.")

Remember that you are competing with college grads
and postgrads for work, so don't be overly choosy. Accept
a job filing or sealing boxes if it's in a place where you
can learn about the business or the industry or make
a contact. You never know where it can lead.

5. There are all kinds of people who specialize in job
counseling. Traditional advisers are listed in the counseling directory described in Chapter 6; alternative life-

style counselors are listed in Richard N. Bolles's book *What Color Is Your Parachute?* An up-to-date directory of counterculture advisers can be found in *Workforce* magazine. (See "Job Exploration" in the Appendix for more information on both.)

If you are planning your stopout a year in advance, consider taking the civil service exam now to qualify for a government job. The government is the biggest employer in the country, and does not ask many questions about how soon you're planning to quit work. Most of the jobs you will qualify for are clerical, but if you know data processing or accounting procedures, you have an advantage. For information, see the free pamphlet *Working for the USA—Applying for a Civil Service Job,* and the other government pamphlets listed under "Job Exploration" in the Appendix.

Women can obtain resume help and job leads from a number of new organizations, including Washington Opportunities for Women (WOW, 1649 K Street, N.W., Washington, D.C. 20006) and Women's Bureau (Washington, D.C. 20210). WOW-affiliated agencies are in Atlanta, Georgia (Atlanta Wider Opportunities for Women), Baltimore, Maryland (Baltimore New Directions for Women), Providence, Rhode Island (Opportunities for Women), Richmond, Virginia (Richmond Women on the Way), Boston, Massachusetts (Wider Opportunities for Women), and Hanover, New Hampshire (WISE-WOW). Women's Bureau has regional offices in Boston, New York, Philadelphia, Atlanta, Chicago, Dallas, Kansas City, Denver, San Francisco, and Seattle.

The Functional Resume

A functional resume abstracts, from your total life experience, the functions you perform well which relate to a particular job goal. It highlights skills and accomplishments instead of specific jobs you have held. It should be used whenever your chronological work experience doesn't support your job objective, whenever you want to deemphasize dates, whenever you want to highlight significant volunteer work, coursework, or hobby involvement that is more relevant than paid work experience.

A functional resume should be neat, clear, and succinct. One page is best. It should include three things: (1) name and where you can be reached; (2) job objective, specifying not a particular job but a general area; (3) a list of your qualifications or skills for the job. These areas of special competence are drawn from your life experience, and should be relevant to the position you're seeking. Examples of "life skills" are: instructing, organization, administration, program development, writing, editing, sales.

You may add a brief educational history or work history (firms, employment dates, positions) if it seems appropriate. But don't include marital status, personal information, pictures, references, or salary expectations. Your goal is to arouse interest that leads to an interview, and times, dates, and places can be filled in on application forms.

SAMPLE FUCTIONAL RESUME

Dana Doe
111 Bridge Street
Littletown, N.Y. 10077
212-888-9990

Job Field Desired: medical laboratory work

Areas of Special Competency:

Care of Animals:
In a summer high school program that was
funded by the federal government and
guided by the Waldemar Foundation for
Cancer Research, Long Island, I was one
of a group of three who researched the
feasibility of using platinum to halt
cancer growth in mice. I became skilled
at injecting the platinum into the tumors,
and was assigned this responsibility.
During the tenth grade my home room was in
the school's biology laboratory. I
volunteered to clean the cages of the
mice, snakes, and other small creatures,
and see that they were provided with food.
I received a commendation for my efforts.

Computer Competence:
I can program in Basic and Fortran II, and
have set up programs using the following
computers: (examples follow). One program
that I devised in high school, which was
for the summer research project mentioned
above, yielded the exact quantity of platinum to be used in injecting mice of minutely
varying weights.

Initiative:
```
I taught myself most of what I know about
computers, since our high school course
covered only the most basic information. In
addition, I taught myself basic electronics
and the fundamentals of electronic music
composition. After taking an electronics
course instituted in my high school, I also
succeeded in building a Paia electronic
synthesizer for the school's use, with grant
money from the Board of Education.
```

Volunteer Work

Volunteer work is valuable experience if you can afford to live without the income, or as many stopouts have done, you can combine your volunteer efforts with a paying job. On the other hand, being supported by your parents while you volunteer your services is an excuse to avoid job-hunting unless you are often too young to find a paying job. In that case, volunteer in a field appropriate to your long-range goals.

If you do opt for volunteer work, keep your stopout goals in mind so you can find an activity that will bring you closer to your objectives. Are you interested specifically in helping young people? There are projects that bring you into courts, prisons, classrooms, and other appropriate places. Is your goal independence? You can volunteer far from home.

An important bonus in volunteer work is getting letters of recommendation. Don't forget to collect these letters at the end of your service period. Laudatory letters are always helpful; letters from successful people in your chosen field will be extremely important when you take the next step after graduation.

Another advantage is your location right on the scene should a paying job open up. (Many women, for example, have moved into paid jobs by first proving themselves invaluable as volunteers.) And if you think you'd like to join the staff on salary once you've got your degree, talk it over *now* with the person in charge.

The following organizations help volunteers find service in their preferred fields or geographic areas:

> Association of Volunteer Bureaus of America
> P.O. Box 7253
> Kansas City, Mo. 64113
>
> Youth Challenge Program
> ACTION
> 806 Connecticut Avenue, N.W.
> Washington, D.C. 20525
>
> United Way of America
> 801 North Fairfax
> Alexandria, Va. 22314
>
> Clearinghouse
> National Center for Voluntary Action
> 1785 Massachusetts Avenue, N.W.
> Washington, D.C. 20036
>
> Neighborhood Youth Corps
> U.S. Department of Labor
> Washington, D.C. 20210

The best directory for volunteers is *Invest Yourself, A Catalog of Service Opportunities,* which is published yearly. It's at your library, or send $1.25 to The Commission on Voluntary Service and Action, 475 Riverside Drive, Room 665, New York, N.Y. 10027. The book lists and briefly describes jobs that pay a little, as well as unpaid opportunities, and covers the United States, Canada, and overseas.

Another route to go: the Alternative Action organizations that have sprung up within the system:

Nader's Raiders
Suite 711, 2000 P Street, N.W.
Washington, D.C. 20036

Medical Committee for Human Rights
542 South Dearborn Street
Chicago, Ill. 60612

National Lawyers Guild
23 Cornelia Street
New York, N.Y. 10003

Union of Radical Political Economists
2503 Student Activities Building
University of Michigan
Ann Arbor, Mich. 48104

Organization of Unemployed Teachers
300 East Santa Inez Avenue
San Mateo, Cal. 94401

Volunteer and Earn Too

This is the ideal compromise for stopouts who want to "do something useful" without piling up debts or depending on parental support. Don't expect a high standard of living; most service jobs pay very low wages. For opportunities, read *Invest Yourself,* or see "Job Exploration: Volunteering" in the Appendix.

If you have a skill, don't overlook VISTA. You'll be provided with only the barest necessities, but the organization will bank $50 a month for you. Apply far in advance; one student told us it took nine months for VISTA to process his application and find him a spot. For VISTA information and applications, phone ACTION in Washington, D.C., toll-free: (800) 424-8580.

Traveling

There are two kinds of travel: putting down roots in one place, and vagabonding. Stopout Jon Mendelson did both. The first time he took to the road, it was to test his self-sufficiency. "I'd never had to boil an egg or think about clean clothes." Since he traveled not so much to investigate the country as to see if he could shift for himself, he first took the quickest, easiest route from Washington, D.C. to San Francisco. His second trip out, his goals were very different: he wanted to see the mountains and deserts, the plains and canyons. So he traveled slowly with a friend. Where you go, how you get there, how long you stay in one place—all will depend on what *you* aim to accomplish.

Many stopouts amass the needed capital before they travel.

> *I worked like a beaver for three months, banked most of it, and made my plans with my bankbook in front of me.* —SALLY TIMKINS

Others prefer to combine spending and earning.

> *I went south and spent a month in St. Augustine working for the county road and bridge department. I took off for San Francisco and found a job there as a bicycle messenger. Along the way I'd stop in a town I liked if I could find a job as a busboy or whatever. I also bought lottery tickets like crazy hoping I wouldn't have to work, but I can't say I recommend that.* —WILLIAM ROBBINS

There are many good books on how to travel and where to stay listed under "Travel" in the Appendix. With the help of ex-stopout Nancy Atlas, the following additional tips have been compiled to update the information in those guidebooks.

1. Think twice about advice from anyone who hasn't been out there *this year*. Successful traveling depends a lot on the state of the economy. Also weigh carefully advice from anyone who's only vagabonded in Europe. There are differences between European and American travel rules, e.g., females shouldn't hitch alone in America, although it's relatively safe in Europe.

2. Be aware of how cold the weather gets. Most stu-

dents forget to plan for this country's sudden weather changes.

3. Figure that every price quoted in a guidebook is out of date; add a 50 percent safety factor. Keep in mind that YMCAs are not all that cheap to stay at. And that sightseeing costs add up unbelievably quickly.

4. When planning to stay at any place recommended by a book, phone your reservation a day in advance. Chances are, a lot of other people are using the same book *you* have.

5. Carry at least twenty dollars cash in untouchable funds. As long as you have that, you can't be arrested for vagrancy. Also, especially if you are male, carry your International Student Identity Card (see details later in this chapter) or another student ID (preferably one with your picture on it) your driver's license, and your registration. If you're under eighteen, bring along a notarized letter from your parents to "whom it may concern" saying they're permitting you to travel on your own during the following months. A letter of introduction from your local chief-of-police is even better. It should contain a phone number to call for verification.

6. Don't count on picking up a job in California, or in any of the popular places that students head for.

7. The easiest place to hitch a ride is a college town. The natives are used to young people, more tolerant, less hostile. If you're near a college, check its ride-board for lifts and share-the-gas deals.

8. When hitchhiking, try to interview the driver before you step in his car. An easy way is to hitch at a highway gas station where you can talk a few minutes at the

pump. While you're at it, offer to share the fuel cost; it's a sure way to get a ride.

9. Hosteling in the United States is usually done on bicycle and by high-school-age travelers. Unlike those in Europe and Canada, American hostels aren't meeting-places for hitchhikers.

10. In towns like Philadelphia and Baltimore, the local rock stations offer free announcements of rides and riders. But if you're female be especially cautious; avoid people looking only for phone numbers.

11. High-schoolers' tour-America groups (like Teen Tours, American Trails, and Trails West) will sometimes feed and offer sleeping space to college students who wander into their camps. Communes will also take you in if you offer to share the work.

12. A last resort: if you're penniless in a big city, find a Travelers' Aid Society. They will help you contact people for assistance, even lend you money. Look them up in the phone book. They also have offices at large airports.

The ISIC Card

In Europe, the International Student Identity Card (ISIC) entitles you to all sorts of discounts on fares, rooms, and even some meals. In America, its chief value is for proof of student status. But there will be times on the road when you'll find that invaluable. And since it's got your photo on it, it will prove that you're a bona fide students entitled to all student discounts; it will also come in handy in identification situations. It's for

sale to "all full-time students engaged in higher education programs (e.g. college, university, vocational school,
secretarial school, etc.) which lead to the granting of a
certificate or a degree and which require a secondary
education as a minimum requirement for entry."

You can obtain the ISIC even if you're on leave of
absence if you enclose with your application form a
*letter from the registrar (or dean or whatever) of your
college granting you a bona fide leave of absence.*
The letter *must* be an original; no Xeroxes accepted.
ISIC will also be issued to students on deferred admission
who can produce (a) the letter of acceptance and (b)
some evidence of payment already made *toward tuition
for the year following your stopout.*

The ISIC costs $2 and is issued by a number of autho-
rized members of the International Student Travel Conference. A good place to obtain it is from SOFA European
Student Travel Center, 136 East 57 Street, N.Y., N.Y.
10022, since they seem most aware, of all the agencies
we contacted, of the ways in which a stopout student
can get a card. If you're not taking an official leave of
absence, buy your card before you leave school. It's
valid until December 31 of that year.

9

Credit While You Work and Travel

THE great difficulty in education is to get experience out of ideas.
—GEORGE SANTAYANA

The Carnegie Commission and the Newman Commission have not only endorsed the concept that students ought to get off campus periodically, but have also urged colleges to begin to recognize the education that results from independent work, travel, and study. A number of schools are taking their advice, and there are now many opportunities for receiving college credits during your stopout.

The most important advantage in using your stopout for credit is time saved toward your degree. In addition, there may be a large immediate money saving. In an era when many schools are charging $200 a credit, a three-credit award is equivalent to $600 in the bank—about as much as you could earn if you worked all summer. Other schools, however, charge fees for awarding stopout credits.

There is a pitfall, however: credits awarded for stopout education are determined arbitrarily. If you later transfer to a different school (even within the same university complex), your credits may be wiped out. Students from Antioch, which has the best-known work-study program in the nation, report that most other schools refuse to transfer their off-campus work credits.

Credits granted by department chairmen are even more difficult to transfer than those earned in college-sponsored alternative programs or exams. To avoid disappointment and confusion should you decide to transfer after you receive stopout credits, ask the dean of admissions of your prospective school about transferability *before* you enter.

Working for Credit

In a growing number of colleges, you are permitted to use your off-campus work experience to earn credits toward the degree. This option is offered either as part of a college-designed educational program, or as a self-directed venture of your own arranging.

Work-Study: A Formal College-Employer Arrangement

College-directed work programs have been around since 1906 when the University of Cincinnati started one, reputed to be the first of its kind in the world. Antioch followed in 1921 and has been introducing variations to the idea ever since. It's sometimes called cooperative education and sometimes work-study—but it has nothing to do with the federal Work-Study Program described in Chapter 5.

Cooperative education means cooperation between the school and firms in the surrounding community. A program is designed in which students alternate a term of full-time work with a term of full-time study. The firm pays the student a wage which increases with his responsibilities. The job is in his area of major interest (although on a low rung of the ladder), and his employer provides an on-the-job adviser who will help him learn. Usually two students alternate at one job so the position is always filled. If a student decides, either because of his work experience or his schoolwork, to change his major, the school will change his job. If he doesn't have a major, the school may let him take jobs in several fields during his work periods, or place him where he can observe a variety of jobs.

Sometimes the student works quite far from campus. Antioch, as a forerunner in work-study, has set up field-study centers in New York, Washington, and California. Other schools aren't as ambitious, but for many students work-study is a legitimate way to get off campus for long periods of time while still working toward a degree.

In the best work-study programs, the jobs are tailored to the people who hold them, the work is progressively more challenging, and the students are supervised by employers who are as interested in education as they are in hiring inexpensive labor or in recruiting future personnel. Work-study students are often invited to remain with the company after they graduate, thus approaching the job market with a two-year lead on regular graduates in terms of wages and responsibilities.

When you're paid the going rate, the school calls it "work-study" or "cooperative education." When you're earning less—and perhaps getting more intensive training on a higher level of professional responsibility—the college usually dubs it "internship"—or even "externship." When you're an education major at almost any school, you work for no pay and it's called "teacher training."

The number of schools offering work-study programs increased from 65 in 1961 to 576 in 1974, with another 245 schools planning or about to implement programs. According to educator Patricia Cross, the idea of leaving school to work, and leaving work to study, is the shape of things to come.

Some colleges offer work-study plans in all their departments, others in only a few. Some schools offer no credit toward graduation for the work—Northeastern (Massachusetts), Louisiana State (Louisiana), and Cornell (New York) are examples. Some, among them Howard, M.I.T., and Wayne State, simply add the work-credits to the usual number they require for the degree. (Most of the latter are five-year undergraduate plans.)

There are, however, many colleges that credit your work toward the degree and graduate you within the normal four years. They are listed in the booklet *Undergraduate Programs of Cooperative Education in the United States and Canada,* prepared for the National Commission for Cooperative Education by the Cooperative Education Research Center at Northeastern University. A copy of the booklet (which also lists two-year colleges with work-study programs and four-year schools on five-year work-study) is available free from the National Commission for Cooperative Education, 360 Huntington Avenue, Boston, Mass. 20115.

Designing Your Own Work-Study

In the programs discussed so far, the school—or an organization acting for the school—chooses your job. Opportunities also exist for the student who wants to develop his own work-study project.

A number of schools have established surprisingly flexible policies of giving credit for work-study experience you arrange yourself, which many colleges call field study or field service. All they require is that you find a supervisor, someone of stature on the job, who will submit a written report on your learning and performance. Usually, you are expected to take the initiative to clear your project with the school beforehand, and then to submit tangible evidence of having learned the equivalent of a semester's worth of some kind of knowledge. If you don't obtain prior permission for your work-study, you may not earn credit for it.

The following is a sampling of colleges that permit you to fashion your own work experience for credit:

Antioch (Ohio)
Bard (New York)
Beloit (Wisconsin)
Campus-Free College (New Hampshire)
Coe (Iowa)
Empire State (New York)
Evergreen State (Washington)
Experiment in International Living:
    School for International Training (Vermont)
Franconia (New Hampshire)
Goddard (Vermont)
Haverford (Pennsylvania)
Hofstra: New College (New York)
Keene State: Alternative One (New Hampshire)
Manhattan Community (New York)
    (an A.A. program)
Michigan State: Justin Morrill (Michigan)
New College (Florida)
Oakland University: New College (Michigan)
Ottawa (Kansas)
Pacific Oaks (California)
Stanford (California)
State University of New York:
    Old Westbury (New York)
State University of New York:
    Stony Brook Experimental College (New York)
Thomas Jefferson (Michigan)

University of Connecticut:
  Inner College (Connecticut)
University of Green Bay (Wisconsin)
University of New Hampshire:
  Life Studies Program (New Hampshire)
University of Puget Sound (Washington)
University of Redlands: Johnston (California)
Washington International (District of Columbia)
Western (Ohio)
Yankton (South Dakota)

Kirkland College in New York was founded for women in 1968 as a companion to its all-male neighbor college, Hamilton. Like most very new schools, Kirkland's 1974-75 catalog is unorthodox in appearance and content. Its section on work-study contains several thoroughly delineated examples of actual projects. The following is taken from a work-study evaluation for which the student received three credits:

> This work/study was based on a job at the Academy of Natural Sciences of Philadelphia. . . . I was hired primarily to do cartographic and drafting work for a report to the National Science Foundation on the Delaware Estuarine Marsh System. . . . I was able to do some research, assist on field trips and help in the lab. . . . In addition to the tremendous amount I learned about drafting and map work, regional planning and limnology, I gained a valuable understanding of organizing material for publication . . . dealing with professionals on their level.

The experience of a pre-graduate job of this type has done much to clarify my feeling about being in college and earning a degree as well as to reinforce my attitudes toward science. . . .

The following is excerpted from the evaluation by her supervisor:

Her responsibility . . . was to organize [the biological information], display it on maps and prepare descriptive text for each map. With respect to land use and environmental impact, she participated in information collection as well as compilation, interviewing officials of state, local, regional and federal agencies and extracting the useful data from their files. She showed such good judgment in separating the important from the unimportant and could be relied on to work independently in this phase of the project as well as in the mapping and tabulating activity, which she did with only minimal supervision. . . . Her performance was outstanding. . . . I would be delighted to have her return here any time, as staff member or student.

Applying for Stopout-Work Credit

One of our stopout interviewees had been the first in his school to design his own work-study stopout plan for subsequent credit. He advises the following preparation:

1. Write a proposal which includes (a) the job you will be doing; more specifically the organization you will

work for, your immediate supervisor, and *all* your job responsibilities; (b) your work/study sponsor or adviser —a superior who will agree to supervise your progress and deliver a written report; (c) your educational goals for the job: learning to operate a lathe? learning to edit a newspaper? Make your goals as specific as possible, and omit goals that aren't *educational*—bettering your emotional or financial state is a worthy personal goal, but neither one is a credit-earning activity.

2. Find someone in your school with the authority and interest to evaluate your proposal and your project report. In most schools, the person to see is the chairman of the department most closely related to your work.

3. Show that person your proposal and reach an agreement on how much credit you can earn if you deliver an evaluation, portfolio, examination, or whatever is acceptable to him as proof of having achieved your educational goals. Since you'll be gone a while working on your project, draw up a written agreement to be signed by both of you.

4. At the end of your stopout, see your sponsor with your project results in hand. Make sure both sides of the agreement have been fulfilled, and then file for the credit.

The foregoing procedure may seem like a lot of work. But it's well worth the effort, even if you transfer immediately afterward, because on the basis of the signed contract and your end-of-work evaluations you may be able to pick up the credit at the school you're transferring to.

Life-Experience Credit

An increasing number of colleges grant undergraduate credits for "life experience" or "life learning." The plan was originally designed for people who were returning to college after many years away, but most schools have extended the plan to include ex-stopouts. For a full discussion of life-experience credit, see Chapter 11.

Schools that offer life experience credit, as well as schools with integral work-study programs, will usually consider a post-stopout request for credits. They look for clear and tangible proof of *educational* growth, so be prepared to document your claims.

Additional Work-for-Credit Opportunities

University Without Walls is a cooperative educational plan using the pooled resources of twenty-five colleges. Working for credit is one of the paths to the UWW degree. See Chapter 11 for a full description.

Campus-Free College and *Empire State College* (see Chapter 11) are also innovative schools which offer work-experience credit.

University Year for Action is a federally sponsored program to which a number of colleges subscribe, in which unskilled students can earn up to a year of college credit by working in community-improvement projects. The Year includes training sessions, faculty supervision, job-related seminars, and the expectation of an end-of-year report from the student. It pays room, board, and a token monthly wage. For a free up-to-date list of all UYA's member colleges, write University Year for Action, 806 Connecticut Avenue, N.W., Washington, D.C. 20525.

VISTA Architects. For most VISTA services, you receive no college credit. But VISTA's Community Design Centers, to which its architects and planners are assigned, receive their support from the American Institute of Architects, so volunteers are usually awarded internship credit toward their architecture license exams. See Chapter 8 for the address to write for more information.

The College Venture Program. Some of the participating colleges in this program (described in Chapter 8) offer credit for off-campus job experiences. Colby College, for example, gave six credits in psychology to a student who used his stopout to work in an Augusta, Maine, state mental institution as a counselor's aide, for which he also earned a "substantial salary."

Smithsonian Institution Museum Study Programs for Undergraduates. These are jobs without pay, but the experience is invaluable and college credits are usually given. You sign up for a minimum of twelve weeks and draw assignments in staff-supervised tasks that permit you to learn about specific scientific or American heritage subjects. For one of these coveted jobs you need scholarly competence and good academic standing. Applications are accepted at any time during the year. Write Museum Study Program, Office of Academic Studies, Room 356, SI Building, Smithsonian Institution, Washington, D.C. 20560.

Youthgrants in the Humanities. The National Endowment for the Humanities has special money set aside for "young persons not in school" to do individual research, editing, and writing in the humanities. If you come up with a project thoughtful enough to win one of these grants, you may be paid as much as $2,000 to complete it, and the finished product may earn you college credits when you get back to school. Write Youthgrants in the Humanities, National Endowment for the Humanities, 806 Fifteenth Street, N.W., Washington, D.C. 20506.

National Endowment for the Arts Fellowships. This National Endowment has no age limit on awarding its grants. It does require that you be a United States citizen or permanent resident and that you show serious purpose and exceptional talent in one of the following areas: architecture and environmental arts, dance, art education, literature, music, theater, the visual arts, or the public media. Write Grants Office, National Endowment for the Arts, 806 Fifteenth Street, N.W., Washington, D.C. 20506.

Credit While You Travel

Jane Fields and Diana Grien spent several months following the Hudson River from its widest point below the Palisades up to its tiny Adirondack headspring at Lake Tear-in-the-Clouds. They kept careful geologic and botanic logs along the entire route. Their earth sciences department chairman helped them plan the goals of their trip, reviewed their logs and summary reports when they returned, and gave them not only the agreed-upon four-credit reward but an additional four credits each for "extraordinary accomplishment."

Glenn Zagorin went to an administrator at the Pratt School of Architecture before he stopped out and asked if he could obtain credit if he took a year traveling through the United States and wrote a book-length photographic essay about it. "Possibly," was the answer. "Show me what you've got when you come back to school and include a report tying your project to the arts. You might earn anywhere from two to twenty-two credits, depending on what you've done."

Although many schools now credit on-the-job training in the field of a student's major, they have been much slower to consider the argument that touring America might be just as educational and therefore just as worthy of crediting toward the degree. Until that happens, if you want credits you'll have to prove that your trip is a travel-study—a primarily *educational* venture that ties in closely with at least one course in the school's bulletin. And even then you will get more approval if you design your plan as an "independent study" (see Chapter 11) than if you call it educational travel.

However, travel-for-credit is gaining recognition. For example, Jane E. Sobel, assistant to the dean of studies at Bennington, said, "If a student can make a case for why independent self-directed travel is equivalent to a term at Bennington, the faculty committee may decide to award credit for it."

Sometimes a dean or a committee decides whether to accept your credit claim. But most often the decision

rests with the chairman of the department in which you
intend to earn the credits. In order to assess your travel
experience, these administrators will demand proof of
purpose. They will expect you to prepare a proposal and
carry through most of the same steps demanded for stopout work-for-credit (see Chapter 10).

The following is a sampling of schools that will consider credit requests for independent travel in the United
States and abroad:

> Allegheny (Pennsylvania)
> Amherst (Massachusetts)
> Antioch (Ohio)
> Anna Maria (Massachusetts)
> Bennington (Vermont)
> Colgate (New York) through Colgate II plan
> Cooper Union (New York) art school
> Cornell (Iowa)
> Duke (North Carolina)
> Fort Lewis (Colorado)
> Goucher (Maryland)
> Hampshire (Massachusetts)
> Immaculate Heart (California)
> Jacksonville (Florida)
> Kirkland (New York)
> Lindenwood (Missouri)
> Marlboro (Vermont)
> Muhlenberg (Pennsylvania)
> National College of Education (Illinois) social
>   science department
> Pitzer (California)

Pomona (California) tested by College Level
    Examination Program (CLEP) general exam
Wells (New York)
Westminster (Missouri)
Wittenberg (Ohio)

A few schools—American International (Massachusetts), Bradley (Illinois), and Smith (Massachusetts)—credit only overseas independent travel.

Don't be disappointed if *your* college administrators still view unsupervised travel as sounding more like "fun" than "education," no matter how much real knowledge about people and geography you expect to absorb from it. Try again next year; their attitudes may have changed.

10

Credit for Independent Study

IT is estimated that by the end of the decade more people will be learning from sources outside the established system than in it.

—K. PATRICIA CROSS, "The Learning Society," in *College Board Review*, Spring 1974

Independent study is the ideal goal of education for which all formal classroom study is but a preparation. College is supposed to teach its students not only a few basic facts about each subject, but how to go about getting more facts and forming independent conclusions.

But as colleges have grown larger, and the ratio of

students to teachers has swelled, pedagogues seem to have been devoting less and less time to teaching the art of learning. It was not the teachers but the students who, in the sixties, rebelled against rote education. They formed small on-campus counterclassrooms for studying subjects in depth as their own interests and needs urged them, in small groups or independently.

This movement toward experimentation in independent study became so popular with students that most colleges are now trying to incorporate some form of it into the curriculum. Often, however, it is tightly structured and closely supervised, an exercise that bears more resemblance to the old-fashioned "honors" courses than to true deep exploration into a topic of interest.

In most colleges when you enroll for a numbered independent-study course, there are restrictive prerequisites; you are usually confined to campus and expected to pursue your project essentially in the school library stacks. In many schools you can't even elect it until your senior year, or unless you have a certain IQ or SAT score. In some you must confine independent study to your major subject; in others you can only take it in fields outside your major.

Often, independent study is an unadvertised offering, hidden in the fine print in the catalog. In some colleges it is referred to as fieldwork—and if you see that term, you're in luck. *Fieldwork* usually implies that you'll be permitted to track down sources of information wherever they are, even off campus. It is closest to being true independent study when you can get off campus, and when the college expects you to devote a large portion of your time to it. When it's a three-credit course offered for a few hours a week, beware: bear in mind that true independent study is anything but superficial.

However, my survey disclosed that most schools are willing to consider the possibility of a student's doing off-campus independent study while on leave of absence. There are only two stipulations: you are expected to pay the usual fee for credits earned in this manner, and you are required to obtain a faculty member's approval and sponsorship. It is often difficult to find a willing and capable sponsor. Equally difficult is achieving a high degree of accomplishment; independent study is often token independence or undirected, chaotic freedom. Accepted independent-study proposals have included such questionable projects as studying marriage (one's own) and a semester of "body massage." At schools where on-campus students earn credit for skiing and yoga, this may seem equitable. But if you decide in the future to transfer to a less eccentric campus, these credits may well be disallowed.

Dressel and Thompson, in their book *Independent Study*, point out that although such study is the intended goal of all higher education, nothing in traditional college courses teaches a student how to undertake such a project. They suggest that the ideal path to *your* independent study should include, in the following order:

1. A course in which class meetings are reduced and the number of oral and written reports increased.

2. A course in which some of the classwork is done outside class.

3. A course in which individual projects can be developed, beyond course requirements, for additional credits—with help available in developing self-confidence and self-direction.

4. A course in which all requirements are completed without class attendance.

5. A special independent project as an extension of a course, for extra credit, with several tasks and specific goals.

At the end of this series of steps, you would be totally prepared for an off-campus independent study, complete with objectives and criteria for evaluation, alone or with faculty help. Unfortunately, say the authors, very few—if any—schools offer such a complete educational package. Antioch's bulletin indicates that it does, and Hampshire, New College, Evergreen State, and the University of Santa Cruz reputedly have well-planned independent study.

How to Get Credit for Independent Study

Three-fourths of the credits for a university degree in Wisconsin can be earned through Independent Study, says a University of Wisconsin extension division flyer. Since the availability of off-campus independent study is sometimes the best-kept secret on campus, you'll have to hunt it down. The first person to query is the instructor or chairman of the appropriate department, although some schools have special independent-study committees, or handle requests through academic policy committees. Other schools expect the dean or the student's adviser to deal with such requests.

Although points can sometimes be picked up *after* the stopout, try to submit a proposal *in advance*. You should also be aware that some colleges expect these proposals to be submitted as much as a semester before you start. A proposal should include:

1. *A title and brief description of the project.* Include what you will do, your objectives in doing it, and why you feel it's a valuable project. If it's related to a course given in the school, indicate the course title. If it's not, explain why you feel it's educationally sound.

2. *Major objectives* of your study: immediate, intermediate, and ultimate.

3. *Procedures to be used.* Include enough detail for your sponsor to assess their validity, reliability, and appropriateness. Include relevant observations to be made and information to be acquired. (A procedural time schedule or itinerary will dispel the doubts as to "seriousness of purpose" which play a large part in faculty resistance to requests for independent study credit.)

4. *People and/or facilities to be used.* Include addresses, phone numbers, titles, and other proofs of qualification. Make certain beforehand that they'll be available to you.

5. *Criteria for evaluating* the completed project, such as time spent, materials used, information gained, skills

acquired, quality of the final product. (All too often, credit is assigned solely on the basis of facts learned.)

6. *Specific evidence of accomplishment* to be supplied by you: reports, tests, portfolios; written and/or oral evaluations.

7. *Suggested credit value* to be received.

Lest you think independent study is a way to gain easy credits, we have excerpted from the Empire State College bulletin an example of two successive independent-study contracts, each worth a year's credits:

> Bob's goal is to pursue a B.A. degree in Psychology with an emphasis in drug prevention programs. . . . Bob's initial contract deals with two areas: the psychology of the drug abuser and addict, which Bob had requested, and the origins of classical Greek culture, which the Mentor introduced as a new element. He felt that Bob had too narrow a base of experience on which to rest the curriculum of his entire undergraduate study.
>
> To broaden his awareness of Greek culture, Bob will read, *The Iliad* and chapters of the pre-Socratics in Windelband's *History of Philosophy*. He will also do research on non-western antecedents of Greek classicism and the tradition of the Orphic Myth. This section of study will conclude with an analytic paper on the non-western and non-linear influences underlying western rationalism.
>
> The second part of the contract is designed to

evolve for Bob new ways of perceiving drug programs and therapy. He will write about his clinical experiences [he'd worked in a drug-treatment program] for one month, using the perspective of one of four different authors: (1) the psychosomatic approach, G. Groddeck, *Book of the It*, (2) the existential-Piagetean-psychoanalytic-literary approach, M. Sechehave, *Autobiography of a Schizophrenic Girl* and *Symbolic Realization*, (3) the psychoanalytic approach, S. Freud, *The Wolf Man*, and (4) the psychopolitical approach, F. Fanon, *Wretched of the Earth*.

In addition to doing these assignments, Bob will also keep a diary of his activities, thoughts, and feelings.

For his second contract, Bob will . . . consider "the history, the poetry, and the chemistry" of wandering as he prepares to travel by the Mediterranean Sea, first to Spain.

To investigate the learning and wandering experience, Bob will read Clancy Sigal: *Going Away,* and M. Twain, *Innocents Abroad.* To develop an understanding of some of the village cultures, he will observe in Andalusia and Italy . . . to understand the historical role of such cultures in modern European and American reformist and revolutionary movements, he will study E. Hobsbaum's *Primitive Rebels.* To develop folklore, collecting, and archaeology skills, he will continue to attend an area workshop in which he will read: [five books].

In preparation for the visit to Spain, Bob will read: [five books].

Finally, he will take the recorded six-week "Living Language" Spanish course, as well as keep a log of his reactions in his diary.

Bob will be spending some of his time in Spain learning Spanish; some of his time working at Spanish archaeology and culture; and some of his time understanding the history of the Mediterranean, particularly Greek history. He . . . will work from a reading list [28 books are listed].

The Continuing Education Unit: Help for Independent Learners

When it comes to awarding credit for independent study, travel, or work efforts, each college is a universe unto itself. It affixes credit value to achievements which might be weighed totally differently by another school. If you graduate from the school you started in and clear all your independent efforts with its faculty and administrators, this arbitrary assignation of credit value is a minor inconvenience, at the worst. But if, as is increasingly common, you transfer to another college (or even to another division within the same university) you may find most of your hard-earned independent study credits crossed off your transcript.

In an attempt to correct this situation, the National University Extension Association devised a CEU (Continuing Education Unit), a unit of measurement which they hope will someday be accepted by all the colleges in the country. (The entire Southern Association of Colleges and Schools has already adopted its use.) The CEU measures participation in noncredit study, so that it may be offered for credit and entered on a transcript. This credit unit can be easily adapted to measure the kinds of stopout learning covered in these chapters.

The Association's book, *The Continuing Education Unit: Criteria and Guidelines,* explains suggested procedures for (a) determining the number of CEUs to be awarded for a particular activity, (b) evaluating successful completion of an activity, (c) establishing and maintaining permanent records on CEUs awarded, and (d) developing and implementing evaluation methods. The book is available for $5.00 from the National University Extension Association, One Dupont Circle, Suite 360, Washington, D.C. 20036.

Planning Your Independent Study

The easiest kinds of learning experiences to get credit for are those which the colleges themselves provide. Languages, arts, archeology, music, crafts—any course in the college bulletin can be studied on your own if you have the interest and tenacity.

Or you can study skills that many schools will not credit toward your graduation but that will put you ahead on the job line: computer training and data processing, accounting, management training, shorthand, typing. A 1974 study indicated that, despite the job slump, graduates who had had engineering, accounting, or business-related courses were in demand. "The people with the worst prospects were recent college graduates with no specialized skills," read a follow-up report.

Or you can study skills that will ease your economic strain throughout school. For instance, an enterprising student who can tune a piano will work fewer hours and earn up to three times as much as the student on federal work-study who earns minimum wage.

How to Learn

> *The idea is that students ought to take responsibility for their own education. The assertion is that you can start learning anywhere. . . . The assumption is that you are capable of making an open-ended contract with yourself to do some learning, and capable of playing a major role in evaluating your own performance. The claim is that if people, students, faculty, and administrators work with each other in these ways, the finest quality education will occur.*
>
> —from the catalog of San Francisco Experimental College

There are as many ways to learn as there are systems for storage and retrieval of information. Some methods are solitary, some communal. Some are traditional, involving tests and measures of your progress. Others are untestable, and often unmeasurable. It's important to choose the learning method that will be most productive and rewarding for you, taking into consideration that *skills* (a statistics course, for example) need no outside aid, *social arts* (i.e. foreign languages) are usually learned better by practicing with a partner, and *theoretical* subjects (physics, for instance) may require a mentor who can answer the mass of questions that arise as you learn.

Solitary Study

The Inexpensive Way

The lowest-cost way to learn is to choose a topic, buy or borrow the books, records, tapes, and other materials needed, and get started. It requires the disciplined dedication that few of us have. But I know a sixteen-year-old who learned three computer languages and an entire basic electronics course this way; if you are excited about your interests, you will probably persevere.

The Oldest Way

There are thousands of things one can learn by mail, and two kinds of correspondence schools to learn them from. The best known are the commercial home-study schools, which teach everything from piano tuning to zoo keeping. For a free complete list of the courses taught and the private home-study schools that teach them, request the most recent *Directory of Accredited Private Home Study Schools* from the National Home Study Council, 1601 Eighteenth Street, N.W., Washington, D.C. 20009.

The other kind of correspondence school can be found within the higher-education establishment. Its courses range from marriage and the family to industrial purchasing. The State University of New York, for example, offers ninety-two correspondence courses through its Empire State College independent-study program. A complete list of courses and sponsoring colleges, the *Guide to Independent Study through Correspondence Instruction*, can be purchased for $1.00 from the National University Extension Association, Department B-1, One Dupont Circle, Suite 360, Washington, D.C. 20036.

The term *accredited* has two different meanings. The commercial schools are accredited by a trade association approved by the government. But when colleges say they recognize courses taken in "accredited" schools, they are referring to accreditation by the regional college associations, which don't recognize the commercial schools. Even a difficult course taken at a reputable commercial school probably *won't* be accepted by your college for credit unless you pass a challenge exam (see Chapter 11) to prove you know the material.

Considerations about correspondence study:

1. Commercial study is not inexpensive. Courses run from $250 to $3,000. The cost is much less for university home-study. The University of Wisconsin extension division, for example, in 1975 offered a nineteen-assignment journalism course for $64 including texts (for which the University of Wisconsin awarded three credits).

2. In all home-study, you can enroll at any time during the year. But universities impose a time requirement, usually twelve months, for completing the course. And

some of the newer college correspondence courses (for example, from the State University of New York) include required end-of-course tests on campus or in designated places around the state or country. This has the advantage of encouraging you to complete your course of study, but you may consider it unwanted pressure.

3. All correspondence courses, even those given by state universities, are open to people of any age (even high school students, in many cases), anywhere in the country, almost without exception.

4. Don't assume that because a college offers credit for a correspondence course it sponsors that your own school will also grant credit. Check with your college, even if you're on leave now, *before* you sign up.

5. Sometimes full-time matriculated students are permitted to take correspondence courses as part of their credit load—especially if they are attending a state college that sponsors a home-study program. It's an alternative worth keeping in mind.

6. While some home-study courses are very good, others are not, and caliber may vary from course to course even within the same correspondence school. The accrediting body approves the school as a whole, not every course. (An *un*accredited commercial school, or one claiming accreditation with any agency other than the National Home Study Council, is to be approached very warily.)

7. Two courses with the same title may cover very different material, so it's important to know what the lessons include *before* you sign up. Also check to see that the lessons are clearly written at *your* level of understanding.

8. Move slowly into any agreement with a commercial school. Even some accredited schools that offer fine courses with honest descriptions have been in trouble with the law for false or misleading advertising and high-powered sales tactics. Though the school's credentials may sound impressive (Macmillan owns LaSalle, and Bell & Howell owns International Accountants Society), you still should not sign without a clear understanding of what you're getting and what your obligations are. A signed application usually becomes a *legally binding* contract when accepted by the school, and you can't get out of a contract as easily as you dropped that college course. Your local Consumer Affairs Bureau* will double-check the school's reputation in your vicinity. (Beware particularly of schools operating entirely within Tennessee, Georgia, or Florida, states that have no regulatory statutes.)

9. Ignore all promises. No school can deliver jobs, success on civil service exams, or positions for which licenses or resident training is required. And some jobs, like airline hostessing, are employer-trained; you don't need a course to qualify. For example, LaSalle never mentioned that its law course would not qualify a person for the bar exam until the Federal Trade Commission got after it. And the Accountants Society offered an "up-to-date" office-management course last year which had been last revised in 1963, before computers took over the offices and revolutionized management techniques. Also ignore "VA-approved" claims. The Veterans' Administration

* The Better Business Bureau is a trade association supported by business and industry. The Consumer Affairs Bureau is a federal agency.

doesn't actually "approve" home-study courses, but relies on state agencies, which are often lax.

10. Only 12 percent of the students who sign up for correspondence courses ever complete them, a far greater dropout rate than college or high school dropout figures. While it's not the fault of the school, it attests to the weighty truth that only the well-motivated, self-disciplined person can be expected to get his money's worth from home-study.

Three New Ways to Study Alone

1. If you're enterprising, you can purchase entire kits of *programmed instruction* for do-it-yourself learning. They differ from home-study in that the only one who checks your lessons is yourself. Although some instruction kits require teaching machines, many don't. Courses are available in banking and finance, business machine operation, blueprint reading, modern math, biology, and other subjects. Originally developed for on-the-job training, they are good for self-teaching *if* a member of your school's faculty will agree to test you after you have completed the course. (See discussion of challenge exams in Chapter 11.)

Information on programmed instruction in your particular area of interest can be obtained from:

Department of Audiovisual Instruction
National Education Association
1201 Sixteenth Street, N.W.
Washington, D.C. 20036

Educational Media Branch, Office of Education
U.S. Department of Health, Education and Welfare
Washington, D.C. 20202

2. Or try a *cassette course*. With this new tool you can learn almost anything. The University of California's University Extension began in 1975 to offer a series of credit-courses-by-cassette which are being made available through local libraries. (For information, write University Extension, University of California, San Diego, Cal. 92037.) Some commercial companies that make teaching cassettes (and will supply title lists and prices) are Xerox Learning Systems, The Executive Voice (a division of *Fortune* magazine), Charles E. Merrill Publishing Company, and Automated Learning, Inc., of Bloomfield, New Jersey.

3. Our old standby, the *library*, is itself being turned into a new resource for independent learners. Under the auspices of the College Entrance Examination Board, a national network of Independent Study Centers is being established in libraries from California to New York. As of 1975, ten library systems had joined the experiment, in which librarians are trained to provide counseling, guidance, and a learning environment for adult students of all ages who are studying a subject, whether for credit or not. Thus far the experiment's membership includes the library systems of Atlanta, Georgia; Cleveland, Ohio; Denver, Colorado; Baltimore, Maryland; Miami, Florida; Portland, Maine; Salt Lake City, Utah; Tulsa, Oklahoma; Woodbridge, New Jersey; and Worcester, Massachusetts. For further information, write to the Office of Library

Independent Study, College Entrance Examination Board, 888 Seventh Avenue, New York, N.Y. 10019.

Study with Others

Apprenticeship

The oldest way to study is with someone who is practicing the craft or skill you want to learn. You can either fill an established apprenticeship position or find someone you respect and apprentice yourself to him. If you're interested in joining ongoing apprenticeship programs, there are many to choose from. (See "Apprenticeships" in the Appendix for reference works.)

If you want to learn something like glassblowing or blacksmithing, consider apprenticing yourself in one of the craft unions. "Apprenticeship," according to a recent *New York Times* report, "had a somewhat greater effect in raising earnings than college education." You will have to sign on for at least two years (and up to six years in some trades), but you will receive a guaranteed weekly wage that increases in steady increments, on-the-job training from experienced craftsmen, and classroom instruction as well. Your local state employment agency has the address of your state's Apprenticeship Information Center, or write for the booklet *The National Apprenticeship Program* available from the Bureau of Apprenticeship and Training, Manpower Administration, U.S. Department of Labor, Washington, D.C. 20212.

Adult Education

Investigate night school or weekend school, which offer courses Friday evening, Saturdays, and Sundays. Most universities, many colleges, and even some junior colleges have a wide variety of subjects for nonmatriculated students. You can usually find a course somewhere in any subject you can think of, from welding to Chinese literature. At Mount Saint Mary in New York, any student over twenty-one can enroll in Friday-Saturday College and pick up a B.A. degree in just four years from start to finish.

There are also evening and weekend courses in business and trade schools, industrial training programs, and hospital teaching centers. (See "Adult Education" in the Appendix.)

Some communities offer adult-education courses under the aegis of local primary-education school districts. If you clear it first with your home college, you may find they'll accept one of these courses for credit.

Electronic Education and the Media

For years the Educational Television Network has been beaming into classrooms from kindergarten to college, offering everything from atomic physics to Russian studies. Most universities have their own radio and/or cable TV stations which carry programs on campus; more and more, these courses are also being made available to people in surrounding communities. For example, the Uni-

versity of Wisconsin has television and radio stations that
offer courses for credit; Chicago TV College has been
awarding associate degrees for fifteen years; and New
York University has been airing "Sunrise Semester" at
6 A.M. every morning for over seventeen years.

Some schools have pushed electronic education even
further, using television, radio, movies, slides—even, in
one case, conference phone calls. Wisconsin University
uses the telephone to teach a variety of subjects, from
library science to pharmacology, and—with the addition
of an Electrowriter, which transmits visual material over
the phone—for courses in engineering and economics as
well.

In 1974, the University of California at San Diego,
with a grant from the National Endowment for the
Humanities, put together three courses on American civili-
zation (to commemorate the bicentennial) for free distri-
bution to every citizen through participating daily
newspapers. The courses have run in every state but three;
and supplementary readings, study guides, and tests are
available at a small charge. For an additional fee, you
can sign up with a participating college to attend seminars
and be awarded credits. (For information, contact: Caleb
A. Lewis, University Extension, University of California
at San Diego.)

Be sure to investigate the universities near you for
their offerings in off-campus education. Contact the
schools' offices of continuing education or extension di-
visions for information. (Administrators in the on-campus
undergraduate colleges of these universities may be una-
ware of these programs. Once they are apprised of them,

they are often willing to evaluate the courses for possible credit.)

Culture Center Courses and Projects

Many museums offer a roster of fine courses, which are taught by leaders in their fields. (For example, Margaret Mead lectures in New York's Museum of Natural History.) The appropriate faculty member at your school may be happy to award credit for such a course.

The Smithsonian Institution offers undergraduate students the opportunity to do supervised research on projects either proposed by them or by Smithsonian staff members (a few scholarships are available to outstanding students). You may apply any time but are expected to stay from at least twelve weeks to a year. Write, giving details about your college background and field of interest, to: Office of Academic Studies, Room 356, SI Building, Smithsonian Institution, Washington, D.C. 20560.

Don't overlook art schools, music conservatories, dance and theater schools, and road companies, many of which welcome qualified students. In addition, consider the travel-study courses (see Chapter 9).

Help in Finding Educational Resources

The Office of New Degree Programs of the College Entrance Examination Board has been helping to develop a nationwide network of information and counseling services specifically for people who are looking for alternatives in higher education. The following member agencies can guide you in evaluating your accomplishments and finding resources for the kind of learning you'd like to pursue:

On Your Own, Denver Public Library
Denver, Col. 80201
(303) 573-5152 ext. 288

Capital Higher Education Service, Inc.
275 Windsor Street
Hartford, Conn. 06120
(202) 527-5261

Study Unlimited, Chicago Public Library
78 E. Washington Street
Chicago, Ill. 60602
(312) 269-2900

Thomas A. Edison College
1750 North Olden Avenue
Trenton, N.J. 08638
(609) 292-8092

Regional Learning Service
405 Oak Street
Syracuse, N.Y. 13210
(315) 477-8711

New York City Regional Center for Life-Long Learning
Pace College
Pace College Plaza
New York, N.Y. 10038
(212) 285-3210

Regents External Degrees
State University of New York
99 Washington Avenue
Albany, N.Y. 12230
(518) 474-3703

Life Experience Center
Edinboro State College
Edinboro, Pa. 16412
(814) 732-2800

Career Education Project
900 Howard Building
Providence, R.I. 02903
(401) 272-5300

Project ARISE
Adult Education Department
396 Smith Street
Providence, R.I. 02908
(401) 272-4900 ext. 241

For more information, write to John R. Valley, Director, Office of New Degree Programs, College Entrance Examination Board, 888 Seventh Avenue, New York, N.Y. 10019.

11

Credit
for What
You Already
Know

WHAT you know is more
important than *how* you learned it.

—NEW YORK STATE REGENTS BROCHURE

A student at Wittenberg College in Ohio was able, on the basis of qualifying exams, to earn his degree in a year and three months of on-campus study.

A student at the State University of New York got his B.A. without ever enrolling in a classroom course.

At the University of Utah, over 1,300 students trimmed a full year from their bachelor's degrees by exams alone. At Newark State, of 400 entering freshmen who took special tests, 90 percent earned some credits and 25 percent immediately became sophomores. At over a thousand colleges, you can gain credit for what you know —or what you learned during your stopout—via tests. For anyone who is concerned about "losing time" in a stopout, credit-by-exam may be a solution.

Credit by AP

If you're still in high school and considering a stopout, your first choice in getting credit for what you know should be the Advanced Placement (AP) program of the College Entrance Examination Board. Most commonly, students prepare for this program by enrolling in college-level courses offered in their high schools; at the end of these courses, they take the AP tests. Depending on the policies of their chosen colleges, the students may be able to count these courses toward the college degree.

AP tests are three-hour exams given in the five classic disciplines (humanities, languages, social sciences, math, and sciences); and they are open to anyone, not only those who have taken AP courses. So consider taking the tests even if you're already out of high school and into a stopout. Send to the College Entrance Examination Board for its course description booklets, at $1 a copy, which explain the syllabi, with sample questions and answers, and list the colleges that grant credit or placement.

A great many high schools are now offering AP classes —although in some you're only permitted to enroll if you've maintained a phenomenal average in all subjects. If you're still in high school and thinking of stopping out later on, keep in mind those college level courses. AP credits have enabled many students to enter as sophomores, take a year's stopout, and still graduate in four years.

While the College Board makes up and grades the tests, its member colleges have never agreed on a uniform credit-recognition program. Therefore, one college may grant credit for a score of 2, another school may reject anything under a 4, and a third may not award any credit —although it will exempt "qualified" students from introductory courses. Some colleges do make exceptions to their stated policies—so you won't know where you stand until you ask.

A few schools insist that you take, during orientation, a "validating exam," which is essentially a repeat of the test you've already taken; and some require a college "validating course"—in effect, the same syllabus you already passed. So you must ask searching questions of any representative who claims that his school accepts AP credits.

Because of conflicting attitudes toward Advanced Placement tests among its member colleges, the College Board publishes a booklet which enumerates, college by college, the lowest grade accepted in each subject for credit, advanced placement, or both, and to whom you can write at each school for further clarification. It also lists over one hundred colleges that are willing to grant sophomore status to students who can pass three or four AP exams. The booklet, *College Advanced Placement Policies*, is available in many libraries and guidance offices, or send $2.50 to College Entrance Examination Board, Box 592, Princeton, N.J. 08540.

You have nothing to lose by taking an AP exam; you can take it over, and you can delete one grade or all on any report you want sent to a college. To take APs if you're not in high school, write to College Entrance Examination Board, stating the tests you plan to take and the school last attended, for a list of the nearest schools administering AP exams. They are given every May.

Credit by CLEP

The College Level Examination Program (CLEP) was conceived in 1967 specifically for the college student who could acquire knowledge outside the formal classroom, and is therefore made-to-order for the stopout.

CLEP tests are totally multiple-choice and about one-third as long as AP tests. There are two catagories. The CLEP general exams include four tests of general knowledge (in humanities, math, the sciences, and the social sciences) and a general English composition test; these are based on the general store of information a person ought to have by freshman year. In addition, there are thirty-four subject area tests. These cover specific topics, such as general psychology and introductory business law, rather than general areas, and you are tested on material that would appear on a syllabus for that course. The general tests are scored from 200 to 800, the subject exams from 20 to 80; as with the APs, each college has its own minimum passing grades. Again, you won't lose anything if you don't pass.

There are a number of innovative, time-shortened degree programs which enable students to "prove" via CLEP tests that they have a certain level of broad general knowledge. On the basis of these tests students can skip one or more years of college, thus graduating earlier.

Tom Phillips, the assistant director of admissions at the State University of New York, Purchase campus, suggests that CLEP test results can also validate independent-study or travel-study experiences. The CLEP tests have been used outside of academia by businesses, industries, government agencies, and even certain professional groups, especially in such areas as computer programming and marketing. A number of organizations accept CLEP exam results to meet their own educational requirements for advancement, licensing, and admission to further training. If you're working during your stopout, you may be able to raise your earnings or your title through these tests.

For a three-booklet package that includes *CLEP General and Subject Examinations: Descriptions and Sample Questions* ($1), a complete list of *Test Centers and Other Participating Institutions* (free), and a *Registration Guide* (free), send $1 to CLEP, College Entrance Examination Board, Box 1824, Princeton, N.J. 08540. (Most libraries have the booklets in their vertical files.) *The New York Times Guide to Continuing Education in America* (Quadrangle, 1972) also contains a listing of "Institutions that Award Credit on the Basis of CLEP Examination Scores."

The College Entrance Examination Board is presently realigning its AP and CLEP tests so that each subject area will be covered by only one exam; it is also adding new CLEP subject exams and revising its test fees, so check CEEB's most recent brochures before making your plans. If you want to know AP or CLEP credit policies at a particular college, contact its admissions office or counseling and testing office. You must, of course, be matriculated at a college in order for that college to consider crediting you for any of these exams.

You cannot, in most cases, amass a number of credits independently and then apply somewhere for graduation. Colleges generally have residence requirements. These stipulations vary from school to school, but basically they require you to earn a specified number of credits from the school you will be graduating from. This policy insures that the holder of a New York University diploma, for example, will also have had predominantly a New York University education; it also assures the college payment for a certain number of credits. There are new programs, however, that are exceptions to this rule; they are explained in detail in this chapter.

The CPE Tests

New York State has been running its own program, similar to the CLEP, since 1963; its tests are called College Proficiency Exams (CPE) and are given in twenty-seven subjects. For the stopout seeking credit for what he's learned on his own, the CPE tests are ideal. They can be used not only in New York State colleges but also for credit or placement in many schools across the country. They are administered in Connecticut, Illinois, and Oregon as well as in New York, and are open to persons of any age living in the United States or abroad.

The CPE program will send free study guides and reading lists to all who express interest in the tests. Write for the free comprehensive catalog, *Regents External Degrees—College Proficiency Examinations,* to: State University of New York, 99 Washington Avenue, Albany, N.Y. 12210. Or send to the same address for examination content outlines and suggested reading lists for whichever exams interest you.

Armed Forces Courses and Exams

The United States government sells correspondence courses and exams-for-credit through its Defense Activity for Non-Traditional Educational Support (formerly called the United States Armed Forces Institute). These courses and exams, available only to servicemen on active duty or in VA hospitals, are accepted for credit by most schools and colleges. If you are doing military service during your stopout, write for more information on DANTES (formerly USAFI) to: Director, DANTES, 2318 South Park Street, Madison, Wis. 53713.

Many armed forces training courses can be accredited toward the college degree. For information on your eligibility, send a letter with pertinent details to: Commission on Accreditation of Service Experience, American Council on Education, One Dupont Circle, Washington, D.C. 20036.

Departmental Exams

In addition to the foregoing credit-by-exam opportunities, many colleges (especially two-year colleges) permit their faculty to award credit and/or course exemption on the basis of examinations. This option is rarely suggested by a professor; the request must come from the student.

In theory, a student should be able to obtain the syllabus for any course, and after mastering its contents, ask to be evaluated. However, Dressel and Thompson, who studied credit-by-exam practices for their book, *Independent Study*, found that challenge exams—the name commonly given to faculty-administered accreditation tests—are usually discouraged by faculty members.

If you're an ex-stopout attempting to get credit for what you've learned outside, approach the teacher of the course and/or the chairman of the sponsoring department with your request for an exam that's equivalent to the course's final. If you score at least a C (in some instances a B), you may receive exemption or credit.

Life-Experience Credit

It is possible to receive academic credit (up to 30 units) for appropriate learning experiences that have taken place outside the classroom . . . teaching, counseling, research, art or music, film making, extensive travel or reading, community service and

> *work internships. . . . Students who have had rich*
> *learning experiences outside the classroom may find*
> *[this] Credit for Life/Career program a valuable*
> *short-cut to graduation. These learning experiences*
> *are recorded on the transcript as are regular courses.*
> —1974 Bulletin of Immaculate
> Heart College, California

Since many stopouts acquire off-campus experience in the field of their major, life-experience credits may be available to them once they return to school. A likely candidate for this type of credit: a violinist taking his degree in music for the time he's spent concertizing; or a person on his way to an education degree, for his work as a volunteer aide in a Head Start program. Adelphi University, which, like Immaculate Heart, credits up to thirty hours for life experience, counts "traveling . . . reading . . . learning a second language . . . hobbies or interests of educational value" all toward its degree. Empire State College and many other external degree colleges listed in this chapter offer up to two years of credit —often in a three-year degree program—for work and living experience.

The *Guide to Life Experience Assessment,* which explains how life-experience accreditation works at Northeastern Illinois University, points out that life experience does *not* mean life competency but, rather, college-type learning: "For example, a millionaire scrap metal dealer might receive an award of 15 credit hours for his skills whereas a non-certified, non-degreed substitute school teacher might receive 40 or more credits. . . . This disparity exists because people normally attend college to learn how to teach whereas very few colleges train people to be scrap metal dealers. . . ." (The pamphlet is available from the Center for Program Development, Northeastern Illinois University, 5530 North Saint Louis Avenue, Chicago, Ill. 60625.)

Some academicians have reacted strongly against the leniency of a few colleges in awarding life-experience credits; some schools offer credit for experiences arising from a ghetto background or a childhood spent touring Europe. In answer, schools that are accused of "devaluing the degree" defend themselves by pointing to the common acceptance of such nonacademic courses as transcendental meditation and skiing. "The true measure of learning," they maintain, "is not how many facts you know but how well equipped you are to deal with life."

A pamphlet, *Get Credit for What You Know,* has been published especially to help women take advantage of the life-experience option. Send 25¢ for leaflet 56 (published in 1974) to the Women's Bureau, Employment Standards Administration, U.S. Department of Labor, Washington, D.C. 20210.)

The Degree Without a College

As previously mentioned, most colleges have some sort of residency requirement, that is, in order to qualify for the degree, you must spend at least one year, often two years (and at St. Johns, the full four years), in "residence" at the school—not necessarily living there, but definitely

paying course fees. But, a few years ago, a new brand
of degree appeared—the degree without a residence requirement. It has been called the external degree, the
off-campus degree, the degree without walls, the extended degree, the nontraditional degree—each term de-
noting a fine shade of difference from the others, but
all basically similar.

The revolutionary aspect of this new type of degree is
that it certifies *competence*, not credit hours, *knowledge*,
not time spent on campus.

The primary way to attain certification in a given area
is by tests. In addition, some programs include weekly
attendance at "learning centers" or intensive week-long
on-campus seminars. Some have faculty advisers, mentors,
or tutors. Others have simply set up degree-granting
boards whose sole purpose is to evaluate a candidate's
readiness, on the basis of tests, portfolios, and proof of
experience, to be awarded an A.A., B.A., or M.A. degree.
The student's learning takes place at home, on the job, at
a learning center, or a local college—*where* he learns
is unimportant. *What* he learns is all that counts toward
the degree. He can enter the program at any time, study
at his own pace, and complete his studies as quickly
or slowly as necessary (most are twelve-month-a-year
schools). All he needs is a great deal of tenacity and
initiative.

Will an External Degree Be Worth Anything?

Most external-degree-granting colleges are being granted
accreditation as fast as they apply. They report that the

degrees their graduates earn are respected in business and industry, and that law schools and graduate schools weigh their transcripts on a par with those from more conventional schools. One college reported that of eighty-three of its graduates who applied to universities, eight-two were accepted into M.A. and Ph.D. programs.

Can External-Degree Students Receive Financial Aid?

Some programs are expensive; at others, your total cost from matriculation to graduation may be less than $1,000. In any case, if you are a full-time student in an external-degree program—that is, if you are taking four courses or twelve credits at a time—you are eligible to apply for any federal grants and loans provided to full-time students. You are also entitled to an International Student Identity Card and all other student privileges. In addition, states like New York which have state-guaranteed loans of up to $1,500 a year will extend these loans to full-time external-degree students.

Does an External-Degree Student Suffer from Lack of Campus Experiences?

The external-degree student is not necessarily deprived of the benefits of on-campus education. True, there are no provisions made for sports or fraternities. But the friendships sparked by week-long or even weekend seminars can be more rewarding than casual acquaintanceships made on campus. In addition, the student–mentor relationship in many external-degree programs offers a close personal contact not often found in the classroom or lecture hall.

Where Are External-Degree Programs Located?

The new external-degree programs have sprung up rapidly in all parts of the country, so very few educational counselors know much about them. Fortunately, they have been monitored by an Office of New Degree Programs which was established through the joint efforts of the College Entrance Examination Board and the Educational Testing Service. The following selection, listed alphabetically by state, is taken from that office's publication, *Increasing the Options,* and from Cyril O. Houle's *The External Degree.* The degrees offered will be abbreviated throughout: A.A.—Associate in Arts; A.A.S.—Associate in Applied Science; A.S.—Associate in Science; B.A.—Bachelor of Arts; B.S.—Bachelor of Science; M.A.—Master of Arts; M.S.—Master of Science.

California
The 1000-Mile Campus: The nineteen campuses of the California State Universities and Colleges have joined to provide an upper-division external-degree program. They hope to utilize tests, electronic aids, and independent study, but so far the classroom lecture arrangement has been used almost exclusively. The program is designed especially to break the one-campus, four-year sequence and provide for the stopouts who, in the words of Chancellor Glenn S. Dumke, "seem to be some of our most successful students." Information: Consortium of

State Colleges and Universities, 5670 Wilshire Boulevard, Los Angeles, Cal. 90036.

Chico State College Regional Campus Project: This is an external-degree program devised particularly for full-time workers. Information: Ralph D. Mills, Chico State College, Chico, Cal. 95926.

Connecticut

Connecticut Board for State Academic Awards: This is Connecticut's equivalent of the New York State Regents External Degree (see details later in this chapter). It uses New York's CPE tests in combination with CLEP, DANTES, and special assessments of life experience to award the A.A. degree. Information: Board for State Academic Awards, 340 Capitol Avenue, Hartford, Conn. 06115.

Florida

Florida International University: This is a new school, chartered by the Florida State University system, which offers B.A. degrees in the humanities, labor and urban justice, manpower studies, urban and environmental economics, urban sociology, urban politics, general business, and the health sciences and social services. You can enroll if you're a Florida resident and have two years of higher education, or its equivalent as demonstrated by CLEP and other exams. The student plans a program, studies independently or at any college, and proves his progress with CLEP tests. Information: School of Independent Studies, Florida International University, Tamaimi Trail, Miami, Fla. 33144.

Illinois

Spoon River College: Students over twenty-five years of age can enroll at any time and achieve an A.A. in liberal studies in anywhere from two semesters to three years via counseling, placement, independent study, and exams. Information: Dr. John R. Berdrow, Spoon River College, 102 East Elm Street, Canton, Ill. 61520.

Board of Governors' B.A. Degree: Designed for the working adult but open to anyone. A student can earn a B.A. through courses at any or all of five Illinois universities as well as through tests, tutorials, independent study, and credits for life experience. Information: Board of Governors of State Colleges and Universities, 222 College Street, Springfield, Ill. 62706.

Massachusetts

Campus-Free College: This college is licensed to grant the A.A., B.A., and M.A. degrees. The student works on a plan of study with a program adviser who lives in the same area. He then arranges for his own education via courses at colleges of his own choosing, tutorials, independent study, internships, correspondence, or any other way he can devise. Information: Campus-Free College, 466 Commonwealth Avenue, Boston, Mass. 02215.

Framingham State College External Degree Program: The student can earn a B.A. in liberal studies through CLEP, independent study, correspondence courses, life experience, travel, military service, etc. He must be on-campus to attend seminars for at least two weeks during each of three summer sessions. Information: Division of

Continuing Education and Special Programs, Framingham State College, Framingham, Mass. 01701.

Minnesota

Minnesota Metropolitan State College: A year-round upper-two-year college with no campus. Students fulfill a degree contract through independent study in community resource areas (libraries, parks, museums, churches, businesses), under the tutelage of "community faculty"—business, labor, and government people who are paid for their time and talent. Students receive degrees when they can show "demonstrated competence." Information: Minnesota Metropolitan State College, Suite LL90, Metro Square, Seventh and Robert, St. Paul, Minn. 55101.

Bemidji State College External Studies Program: This program offers the A.S., B.A., or B.S. through independent study, with majors in community service, humanities, business administration, accounting, vocational education, industrial technology, criminal justice, and other disciplines. Information: Lorraine F. Cecil, Coordinator, External Studies, Bemidji State College, Bemidji, Minn. 56601.

New Jersey

Thomas A. Edison College: Modeled on New York's Regents External Degree (see below), the college grants the A.A., the A.A.S. in management, the A.A.S. in radiologic technology, the B.A., and the B.S. in business administration, all on the basis of proven competence through courses, exams, and individual assessment of life experience. In addition to its recognition of CLEP and CPE, Edison has begun to develop its own exams and already administers them for five foreign languages as well as business administration. Information: Thomas A. Edison College, 1750 North Olden Avenue, Trenton, N.J. 08638.

Undergraduate Urban Fellows Program: This is a unique experiment directed at "talented and productive individuals." The student defines his learning needs, negotiates a contract with other Urban Fellows and staff, and utilizes courses, seminars, tutorials, CLEP, life experience, independent study, etc., to meet those needs. The consortium of colleges participating in the Urban Fellows Program grows larger every year. Information: New Jersey Education Consortium, Inc., U.S. Route 130 and Hickory Corner Road, Hightstown, N.J. 08520.

New York

Regents External Degree Program: This program has no campus, no faculty, and no instruction. Students from anywhere in the world may qualify with the State University of New York for any of seven degrees (A.A., A.S., A.A.S., or A.S. in nursing, B.A., B.S., or B.S. in business administration) on the basis of CPE, CLEP, AP, and DANTES or USAFI exams, course credits, correspondence, and other independent study, military service school courses, and special Regents External Degree exams— including individualized special assessments. You can take as long as you want (your credits are held in a special "credit bank"), and you needn't have a high school diploma to qualify for admission. This is the most highly developed external-degree program to date, with detailed study guides, complete departmental offerings, and a network of volunteer advisers throughout the state and in other parts of the country. Information: Send for the bulletin, *Regents External Degrees/College Proficiency Exams,* to the Regents External Degree Program, State University of New York, 99 Washington Avenue, Albany, N.Y. 12210.

Empire State College: The student enters at any time during the year and makes a learning contract with his faculty mentor for an A.A., A.S., B.A., or B.S. degree plan. He may use one of a network of learning centers on college campuses throughout the state, and can also use museums, industry, and public agencies for learning resources. He learns through courses, group study, tutorials, independent study, work, travel—and can live anywhere in the world, as long as he can get to New York once a month to meet with his mentor, or find a mentor outside New York. (There is a mentor in London for overseas students.) Empire State College offers, through its independent study program, ninety-two correspondence courses of its own in twelve fields. Information: Director of Admissions, Empire State College, 2 Union Avenue, Saratoga Springs, N.Y. 12866.

Manhattan Community College: The Associate degree is offered to students over twenty-one years of age with three years' full-time work experience; options toward the degree include independent study, credit-by-exam, traditional courses, and life experience. Information: Registrar, Manhattan Community College, 134 West 51 Street, New York, N.Y. 10020

New York Institute of Technology: The B.A. and M.A.

in business administration, and the B.A. in political sciences, behavioral sciences, economics, and technology are all offered through independent study. With the aid of study guides, cassettes, and correspondence assignments, students mail in written work to assigned instructors or turn them in at the four to six weekend seminars held on campus and at regional learning centers. Information: External Degree Programs, New York Institute of Technology, Old Westbury Campus, Wheatley Road, Old Westbury, N.Y. 11568.

Ohio (not limited to Ohio, but based in that state)
University Without Walls: In operation since 1964, the UWW now includes twenty-five participating colleges throughout the country. "Students, faculty, and administrators participate in the design of programs that may involve a mix of regular courses, research assistantships, internships, field experiences, independent study, projects, telelectures, videotapes, programmed learning, and travel," reads a UWW brochure. "There are no fixed time limits [for completing the degree] or curriculums. . . . Adjunct faculty are used. . . . The degree will be awarded by the sponsoring institution or by the Union for Experimenting Colleges and Universities in cooperation with the sponsoring institution." Students are judged on the basis of competence as "liberally educated persons," not grades or credit hours, and can enter at any time during the year.

As of now, the member colleges in the UWW consortium are: Antioch, Bard, Chicago State University, Franconia, Friends World College, Goddard, Hofstra

University, Loretto Heights, Morgan State, New College
at Sarasota, Northeastern Illinois University, Pitzer, Roger
Williams, Shaw, Skidmore, Staten Island Community College, Stephens, University of Alabama (New College),
University of Massachusetts, University of Minnesota,
University of the Pacific, University of Redlands (Johnston College), University of Southern California, University of Wisconsin at Green Bay, and Westminster.
Information: Write directly to any of the participating
schools, or to the Union for Experimenting Colleges and
Universities, Yellow Springs, Ohio 45387. (Each campus
has a slightly different program, so you ought to investigate several before making your selection.)

Pennsylvania
University of Pittsburgh External Studies Program:
Home-study credit courses are combined with telephone
contact with instructors and three on-campus seminars for
each course; in addition, CLEP and challenge exams are
offered. Students may achieve the B.A. or B.S. Information: University External Studies Program, University of
Pittsburgh, 200 South Craig Street, Pittsburgh, Pa. 15260.

College-at-Home Program: Through cassette tapes
and photo slides, testbooks, and self-tests, and consulta-
tions in person and by phone, students take courses at
home toward the Associate degree in arts, science, general education, or applied science. CLEP and challenge
exams are also utilized. Information: College-at-Home-
Program, Northampton County Area Community College, 3835 Green Pond Road, Bethlehem, Pa. 18017.

Campus-Free Degree: The Bachelor of Liberal Studies,

Bachelor of Business Administration, and three Associate degrees are planned for this new program, in which life experience will be weighed for credit by an evaluation committee, and CLEP, correspondence work, and all other learning experiences will also be considered for credit. Information: Center for Community Education, Alpha Hall, Elizabethtown College, Elizabethtown, Pa. 17022.

Utah
Brigham Young University: Through a combination of independent study and three-week seminars, students are guided toward B.A. degrees. Information: Bachelor of Independent Studies, Division of Continuing Education, 222 Herald Clark Building, Brigham Young University, Provo, Utah 84601.

Vermont
Community College of Vermont: Using regional learning centers throughout the state, the college's counselors help the rural population toward the Associate degree. Students are encouraged to explore many areas and to contract with a counselor for an individually designed degree program based on personal needs. Information: Peter F. Smith, Director, Vermont Community College, P.O. Box 81, Montpelier, Vt. 05602.

Proposals for external-degree programs are being considered by many other colleges. There also have been serious suggestions for a National University and an International University, both offering degrees without

campuses. Clearly, the degree-without-a-college option
is no passing fad but an indication of the lifelong stop-
out/stop-in trend that is expected to be the pattern of
the future.

Credit Banks

A number of external-degree agencies, including the New
York State Board of Regents and the California State
Colleges and Universities system, have recognized that if
people are to be given options in their methods of obtaining the degree, there must be some method of evaluation
and of providing transcripts to consolidate their academic
records. These agencies have suggested the establishment
of credit banks. The New York State Regents have theirs
in operation at the present time. For an enrollment form
or more information on the Regents Credit Bank, write:
Credit Bank, Regents External Degree, State University
of New York, 99 Washington Avenue, Albany, N.Y. 12210.

The Regents intend for their credit bank to be used by
individuals who have attended several colleges and who
want to consolidate their record into one consistent,
cumulative transcript "for easy reference for themselves
. . . for admission to college or for employment." For stopouts who take a course here, a course there, and travel in
between, such a transcript could be a great aid in keeping
credits intact. Perhaps the Regents Credit Bank might
serve as a model for a future national credit bank. Such a
credit bank, in coordination with a nationally recognized
continuing education unit, would accredit and officially

transcribe every unit of education a person earns, in school and out, over the years. In that way, those who are mostly self-taught will not be penalized for an individual style of learning.

12

Stopping in Again

WHY go back? To keep your curiosity alive.

—CHARLES DE CARLO

Every few years a book appears asking, "Why go to college?" and concluding, "It's a waste of time." In 1965 it was John Keats's *The Sheepskin Psychosis*, in 1970 Ivar Berg's *The Great Training Robbery*, in 1975 Caroline Bird's *The Case Against College*. For the 30 percent (or fewer) of the college dropouts who never go back, these books provide much support for their decision.

But for most, the message in these books has nothing to do with reality. For a number of reasons, people want, need, expect the college degree. This includes stopout students as well. Returning to school is generally the anticipated outcome of stopping out; graduation is still a desirable goal. The fact is, students who are stopping in constitute the fastest growing population on the American campus.

Why such a strong desire for college education? Perhaps because of the awareness that knowledge is not only valuable for its own sake, but that it tends to change people. Researchers have been able to document, with statistics, that four years of college enhances intellectual curiosity, individualizes one's thinking, makes a person more tolerant of ambiguity, and makes one receptive to a broader range of environmental conditions. The Carnegie Commission summed it up in its report, *Purposes and Performances of Higher Education:*

"College graduates," it said, "do find their jobs better paying and more interesting and their lives more satisfying, do participate more in community affairs, do exhibit more tolerance toward their fellow man, and do engage more in cultural activities. . . . They are generally better able to make the myriad decisions with which the modern American is faced."

The economic benefits, as well as the intellectual ones, are substantial. As Alexander M. Mood points out in *The Future of Higher Education,* most employers still favor college credentials. And according to Mood, this bias will not disappear much before the year 2000.

The vast majority of returning students find that they are relaxed, motivated, and suddenly really interested in their courses. They report a new sense of competence and a clear understanding of themselves in relation to their environment. More than 95 percent were glad they'd left school, but were also glad to be back.

The students for whom stopping in isn't successful are by and large the students who have expected college to change to their specifications in their absence or to make a special effort to welcome them back. Usually the college will provide even less nurturing aid to the stop-in than to the freshman. Advisers still won't help much with program planning or career counseling. Professors will vary in their abilities to excite and stimulate. Deadlines will still be set without directions, reminders, or warnings— even in the reapplication process.

> *I was traveling around the country that spring, and in the fall I was going back to school. Since I was away, I missed preregistration and was closed out of quite a few courses, and the school wasn't making allowances. In addition, the computer messed me up by leaving me off a lot of lists, and there was no flexibility even about the computer's mistake. I guess I had forgotten how disorganized the school administration could be.* —WILLIAM ROBBINS

Be realistic in your expectations and you won't be hit with that sense of frustration that makes a student want to stop right out again. Concentrate on the reasons that made you decide to stop in: your search for answers to intellectual questions, your desire for certification. Find a college that will serve your needs, use it to your best advantage, and accept its limitations.

Finding a College that Fulfills Your Needs

In the words of one ex-stopout: "I dropped out of my first school because I was looking for the perfect college. I tried three schools before I was ready to settle down and work toward my degree. Part of my education has been learning not to expect perfection from any school."

Of course, there are differences among colleges, and if you choose a college which "fits" you well, you're not likely to be yearning for another stopout this time next year. "Fit" will depend on a number of measurements: your major, your style of learning, your competitiveness, your preference in a choice between freedom and structure.

Schools for Your Major

An acquaintance recently told me that his son had stopped out of an Ivy League school only to stop into a state college in Colorado "not because it's strong in his major, but because he fell in love with the scenery out there." That is a good way to choose a homesite, he felt, but not an education.

In choosing a school to stop into, you are at an advantage if you have decided on a major field of interest. For guidance in finding schools that offer your major, peruse the latest edition of Barron's *Profiles of American Colleges: Volume 2: Index to Major Areas of Study.* But keep in mind when using it that it is *no* guide to the *quality* of teaching in any particular department at any one school. A better indication of which schools are especially strong in the area of your major are the faculty lists in college bulletins. Check to see which colleges graduate professors in your area of interest.

Another approach is to write to some well-known people and professional associations in your future field, asking them to suggest schools for you. Enclose a stamped, self-addressed envelope, and you should receive several valuable replies.

Schools for Your Learning Style

The Newman Report suggests that if you stopped out because you felt your grades weren't good enough, it may have been because you are a "nonacademic learner" and need to learn from experience rather than from abstractions. In that case, choose an educational atmosphere that will permit you to engage in research, to work with materials, to spend time using tools.

But you may have discovered during your stopout that you're happiest reading textbooks and publications, attending lectures, questioning and debating theories with a group. If that's true, choose an educational atmosphere that offers lectures, seminars, tutorials. Neither the experience-based curriculum nor the classroom-and-reading method is superior; each person is an individual, and will best succeed with his particular style of education.

Community Schools Versus Four-Year Colleges

The two-year college traditionally served as a "finishing school" for women, and some of the older two-year colleges retain this flavor of a general, well-rounded education. The newer two-year community colleges offer two educational approaches: career programs, which teach marketable trades and lead to the Associate degree; and academic programs, which prepare students to transfer as juniors to four-year colleges. Almost one-third of community-college graduates do transfer directly to four-year schools. Another large percentage stop out with their A.A.s and later come back. Recently, in Florida and California, two-year junior-senior schools have opened, mainly to absorb the post-graduate community population.

There are pros and cons to stopping in at a two-year school. On the one hand, many students lose up to a semester in credits if they go from two-year to four-year colleges (although there are indications that this state of affairs is changing). In addition, Dr. Alexander Astin points out in *Preventing Students from Dropping Out* that because undergrads who live at home have difficulty becoming part of the college community, a greater dropout rate prevails at community colleges. On the other hand, the climate is usually less competitive and grades tend to be higher than at four-year colleges. Spending your sophomore year, and doing well, at a community college may increase your chances for transferring into a really good four-year school as a junior.

But if you're a science major, avoid two-year schools.

Dr. Susan Atlas of Johns Hopkins told us, "Science laboratories at community schools are poorly equipped as a rule. The good four-year colleges will often ask a transferring science major to repeat all his lab courses."

Schools with Innovative Programs

Innovation, expression, and creativity were catchwords of the sixties; in the seventies, students became more oriented toward goals, careers, jobs. Colleges have recently, for lack of student interest, even begun dropping the pass-fail option.

Still, many of the sixties' experiments have survived and prospered. One authority estimated that in 1972 between one-fourth and one-third of the country's colleges were offering nontraditional programs somewhere on campus. Some schools are entirely innovative, like Hampshire, Marlboro, Goddard. There are also innovative programs tucked into odd corners of large university campuses under names like the "new college" or the "experimental college"; the program can consist of anything from student-created lecture courses to independent study. There are "new colleges" at the University of Alabama and at Oakland University in Michigan; "experimental colleges" at Tufts in Massachusetts, at Fresno State in California, at State University of New York at Stony Brook, and on many other campuses.

Other innovative options include three-year degree programs, weekend colleges, and schools with no course requirements, all discussed elsewhere in this book. The twin colleges, Hobart and William Smith in New York, have for several years offered a unique educational package in which you can compress work on the sophomore-junior year level into an intermediate "middle year." At Northern Colorado State, students in a special program do advance reading in a course, attend lectures in the subject for forty hours in one week, and then complete the course with independent papers or exams. Schools are also experimenting with ways to chop the year into learning segments; for example, Colorado College has nine three-and-a-half week "blocks" of coursework and Mt. Vernon College in Washington, D.C. has ten three-week "modules."

In seven states, new public-service centers are trying to keep track of all the educational alternatives. Their personnel are well qualified to help stopins. Their addresses are listed in Chapter 10. (In addition, see the "College Directories" and "Alternative Education" listings in the Appendix.)

Free Universities and Other Counterculture Schools

"New" and "experimental colleges" within larger schools are, for the most part, accredited, as are some innovative schools like Antioch. Another alternative educational setting is the "free university."

Most "free universities," on the other hand, offer no grades, no transcripts, no degrees, and—most important—no accreditation. If you are attending college primarily for the degree, you'll want recognized certification. If your school isn't accredited, other colleges, employers, and even external-degree agencies may not accept its degree as valid. If this is not an important consideration for you, the informal atmosphere of a free learning center may be your best option. Many free universities are free in the financial sense as well. Fees, when requested, are often on a voluntary basis. See "Alternative Education" in the Appendix for more information.

Questions Stop-Ins Ask

Do Stopouts Have Trouble Being Readmitted?

If you want to stop back into your old school, it may soon be as simple as registering for a new term. Colleges are slowly relaxing their readmission policies to the point where, in several schools, a letter of request will get you readmitted. This is true not only of some large public universities but also of small, private colleges. A letter to your school's admissions officer will elicit a response as to its current policy.

Or you may decide to transfer to a new school when you are ready to stop in. Fully 99 percent of the colleges in my survey informed me that they treat all new transfer applicants alike, whether or not they've been stopouts, as long as they seem serious about resuming their studies, and as long as they can account sensibly, in the admitting officer's opinion, for their stopout time.

Is Being Older a Disadvantage?

Sometimes I feel like a twenty-nine-year-old teeny-bopper, but I look eighteen and the other students

*are suprised when they find out I'm married and have
children. Actually it's an advantage being older, because my emotional state is settled. I've gotten
straight A's since I've been back.*

—LEIGH MCCULLOUGH

Most colleges make no special provisions for their older
stop-ins, aside from exempting them from on-campus
housing requirements (and in some cases even insisting
that older stop-ins live off campus). There are exceptions:
schools like the University of Bridgeport in Connecticut
which make it their policy to give special help to their
older students. A growing number of schools have lowered
the tuition fees for people who have been out of academia
at least three years. But generally, the older student's age
is in no way taken into consideration by the school.

Your age may affect your social life if being among your
own peers is important to you. At a school like Amherst
or Oberlin, where most of the population is under twenty-
two, you may feel uncomfortable. But at a university with
a graduate school on campus, your age will not set you
apart from the other students.

If you've married during the stopout, ask the admissions
officer how many married students are in the school,
whether appropriate housing is available, and whether
there are special rules or provisions concerning married
students. Some schools guarantee dual financial assistance
to couples who are both attending classes. At Iowa
Wesleyan, priority is given to married students for on-
campus work-study opportunities. At Antioch, where
work-study terms are often taken far from campus, mar-

ried students can make arrangements so that if there are children at least one parent is scheduled to be on campus.

Most universities have on-campus apartments for their married graduate students, and some have day-care facilities. Married undergrads usually, but not always, will be permitted to take advantage of these facilities.

Has My Financial Aid Eligibility Changed?

Many students quit school because they feel they can't manage the costs of college. In Chapter 5 are reviewed the many loans, grants, and work-study programs set up so that no student need stop out—or stay out—for financial reasons. These aid packages are all available to stopins as well, and some schools even set aside special funds for transfer students. In any case, early application, meaning before mid-term of the semester before your return, will insure you consideration for the resources available.

If you've been living on your own earnings for at least a year, you may be able to qualify for aid as an emancipated minor or self-supporting adult. (See Chapter 5.) In addition, some schools offer half-tuition rates to students who have been out of school for several years. Inquire at the financial aid office.

What If I Want to Stop Out Again?

Most colleges told me you can stop out and in forever, as long as you make your exits official. But in reality, a revolving-door approach to education looks suspicious to many admissions people. So if you do have doubts about the school you're stopping into, do it by degrees. Stop in as a part-time, nonmatriculated, or "unclassified" student; uncover the college's own alternative to full matriculation and use it to test whether the school fits you and you fit it. If after a few courses you realize the fit is wrong, pick up your credits and head somewhere else.

If you find you need to stop out a second time, don't hang on just to save face or avoid problems. Most admissions people are willing to listen to good reasons and are open to evidence of time well spent.

Almost without exception, the stopouts I spoke to all had in common a love of learning, a desire for a degree, and a need to achieve their goals on their own time schedule, in their own fashion. Most of them have already stopped back in; a few, as the end of the semester rolls around, are beginning to think of stopping out again.

Such a learning style may seem aimless, a waste of time. But these students *are* purposeful; they use their time better than most. They stop out to investigate who they are and what they want from life. When they stop back in, many return with answers to those questions. Once they know what kind of education is best for them, they can begin to make use of such knowledge.

Appendix

Adult Education

The New York Times Guide to Continuing Education in America, Frances Coombs Thomson, ed. (College Entrance Examination Board, Quadrangle Books, 1973) $4.95 paper.

National Directory of Adult and Continuing Education, by Steven E. Goodman. (Education and Training Associates, P.O. Box 304-BK, Dunnellen, N.J. 08812) $10.00 paper.

Continuing Education Programs and Services for Women, Pamphlet 10 (The Women's Bureau, Employment Standards Administration, U.S. Department of Labor, Washington, D.C. 20210, 1971) $1.55.

Directory of Postsecondary Schools with Occupational Programs, Public and Private, by Evelyn R. Kay. (National Center for Educational Statistics [DHEW #(OE)73-11410] care of Superintendent of Documents, U.S. Government Printing Office, Washington, D.C. 20402, reprinted 1973) $3.95 paper.

Directory of U.S. College and University Degrees for Part-Time Students, by Robert J. Pitchell. 1973. (National University Extension Association, One Dupont Circle, Suite 360, Washington, D.C. 20036) $1.95.

Alternative Education

This Way Out, by John Coyne and Tom Hebert. (Dutton, 1972) $4.95 paper.
  Describes various experimental colleges.
Five Experimental Colleges, by Gary B. MacDonald, ed. (Harper Colophon, 1973) $3.25 paper.
  Describes and examines Antioch-Putney Graduate School of Education, Vermont; Bensalem College at Fordham University, New York; Fairhaven at Western Washington State, Washington; Franconia, New Hampshire; and State University of New York at Old Westbury, New York.
Guide to Alternative Colleges and Universities, by Wayne Blaze, Bill Hertzberg, Roy Krantz, and Al Lehrke (Beacon Press, 1974) $4.25 paper.
"Colleges with Alternative Forms of Education," in *Barron's Profiles of American Colleges: Volume 2.* (Barron's Educational Series, 113 Crossways Park Drive, Woodbury, N.Y. 11797, annual) $4.95.
Free University Directory, by Jane Lichtman. (The American Association for Higher Education, One Dupont Circle, Room 780, Washington, D.C. 20036; published periodically) $1.50.
Directory of Alternative Schools in the U.S. and Canada (1973–74). (New Schools Exchange, P.O. Box 820, St. Paris, Ohio 43072) $3.00.
  A one-year, twenty-issue subscription to the New Schools Exchange *Newsletter* includes the *Directory* and costs $10.

Workforce magazine (see "Job Exploration—Volunteering") lists learning centers and free-school clearinghouses on its education page in each issue.

Apprenticeships

This Way Out. (See under "Alternative Education.")
Suggests ways to find a mentor.
By Hand, by John Coyne and Tom Hebert. (Dutton, 1974) $8.95.
Lists, by state, more than 750 crafts cooperatives, apprentice programs, centers, and workshops.
Somewhere Else, A Living-Learning Catalog, by the Center for Curriculum Design. 1973. (Swallow Press, 1139 Wabash Avenue, Chicago, Ill. 60605) $3.25 paper.
Lists 400 places that teach skills such as blacksmithing, glassblowing, book-writing, and courses in survival training and nonviolence.

Career Information

Careers for College Graduates. 1972. (College Placement Council, Inc., P.O. Box 2263, Bethlehem, Pa. 16601.
The Career Opportunities Series. (J. G. Ferguson, 6 N. Michigan Avenue, Chicago, Illinois 60602, $6.95 each.)
Books on various fields: marketing, business, health, engineering, ecology, environmental control, etc.
Occupational Outlook for College Graduates. (U.S. Department of Labor, Bureau of Labor Statistics.)
College Courses and Beginning Jobs. (Superintendent of Documents, U.S. Government Printing Office, Washington, D.C. 20402) 15¢.

Federal Career Directory, A Guide for College Students.
1973. (Superintendent of Documents, U.S. Government Printing Office, Washington, D.C. 20402) $2.35.

Paraprofessions: Careers of the Future and the Present,
by Sarah Splaver. (Julian Messner, 1972) $4.95.

College Directories

The College Handbook. 1975 edition. (College Entrance
Examination Board, Box 592, Princeton, N.J. 08540)
$9.50 by mail, $12.50 in bookstores.

Barron's Profiles of American Colleges. (Barron's Educational Series, 113 Crossways Park Drive, Woodbury,
N.Y. 11797, annual) Volume 1, $5.95, Volume 2, $4.95.

Lovejoy's College Guide. (Simon and Schuster, biannual)
$4.95 paper.

Comparative Guide to American Colleges, by James
Cass and Max Birnbaum. (Harper and Row, 1973)
$5.95 paper.

The Insiders' Guide to the Colleges, by the staff of the
Yale Daily News. (Berkley Medallion, New York, fifth
revised edition, 1974) $2.25 paper.

Even if your college choices are not among the
200-odd schools included, a reading of the pros and
cons of various campuses and programs will help your
investigations of other colleges.

Financial Aid

Books

Making It, A Guide to Student Finances, by Harvard
Student Agencies. (Dutton, 1973) $4.95 paper.

Also gives suggestions for employment on campus.

Questions and Answers About Getting Into College, by Abraham H. Lass. (Pocket Books, 1974) $1.95.

Contains material especially useful for minority and disadvantaged students.

Financial Aids for Higher Education 1974–75, by Oreon Keeslar. (William C. Brown, 1974).

Scholarships, Fellowships, Grants and Loans, by Lorrine Mathies. (Macmillan Information Division, second edition 1974) $29.95.

Financial Aids for Undergraduate Students, by Lewis D. Hall. 1970. (College Opportunities Inc., Ohio).

Pamphlets

Need a Lift? (The American Legion, Department S, P.O. Box 1055, Indianapolis, Ind. 46206). 50¢.

This 132-page booklet, revised annually, lists private, state, and national scholarships and loans.

Meeting College Costs. (College Entrance Examination Board, Box 592, Princeton, N.J. 08540) free. Revised annually.

Going Right On, by Carl E. Drummond. (CEEB, above address) free. Steers minority students to a variety of sources of financial aid.

Guide to Student Assistance. (U.S. Government Printing Office, Superintendent of Documents, Washington, D.C. 20402) free.

Financial Aid for College Students, by Richard C. Mattingly. (U.S. Government Printing Office, above address) free.

Goals Exploration

How to Make a Habit of Success, by Bernard Haldane. 1975. (Acropolis Books, Washington, D.C.) $3.50 paper.
Career Satisfaction and Success: A Guide to Job Freedom by Bernard Haldane. 1974. (Amacon, New York) $9.95.

Independent Study

Directory of College Transfer Information, Carl M. Dyer and Gerald B. Flora, eds. (American Schools Association—Simon and Schuster, 1974) $25.00.

Includes an index listing more than 550 colleges that accept correspondence credit on transfer transcripts.

Directory of Independent Study Programs Offered in Colleges, Universities and Private Institutions Throughout the United States and Canada. (Educational Consultants, Inc., St. Louis, Mo.) $4.50

Job Exploration

Books

How to Succeed in Business Before Graduating, by Peter Sandman and Dan Goldenson. (Collier Books, 1968).
How to Earn (A Lot Of) Money in College, by the Harvard Student Agencies. (Harvard Student Agencies, 1968) $1.95.
What Color Is Your Parachute? A Practical Manual for Job-Hunters and Career-Changers, by Richard Nelson Bolles. (Ten Speed Press, Box 4310, Berkeley, Cal. 94704, revised periodically) $4.95 paper.

Go Hire Yourself an Employer, by Richard K. Irish. (Doubleday Anchor, 1973) $2.95 paper.

Executive Jobs Unlimited, by Carl R. Boll. (Macmillan, 1965) $4.95. See Chapters 3, 4, and 6. Describes the "broadcast letter."

The Professional Job-Changing System: World's Fastest Way to Get a Better Job. 1974–75 edition. (Performance Dynamics, Inc., 17 Grove Avenue, Verona, N.J. 07044) $12.00.

Pamphlets

Employment Opportunities in the Bureau of Sport Fisheries and Wildlife, from the Bureau of Sport Fisheries and Wildlife; *Working for the Bureau of Outdoor Recreation,* from the Bureau of Outdoor Recreation; *Park Aids and Technicians,* from the Bureau of Land Management. (Each of these is free from the indicated bureau, care of the U.S. Department of the Interior, Washington, D.C. 20240.)

Women in the Forest Service. (From the Forest Service, U.S. Department of Agriculture, Washington, D.C.).

Working for the USA—Applying for a Civil Service Job, U.S. Civil Service Commission (Pamphlet #4. Superintendent of Documents, U.S. Government Printing Office, Washington, D.C. 20402) free.

Job Exploration:
Self-Employment

Making It: A Guide to Student Finances, Harvard Student Agencies. (Dutton, 1973) $4.95 paper.

Up Your OWN Organization, by Donald M. Dible. 1971. (Entrepreneur Press, Drawer 2750, Mission Station, Santa Clara, Cal. 95051) $14.95.

Subtitle explains further: "A Handbook for the Employed, the Unemployed, and the Self-Employed, on How to Start and Finance a New Business."

Woodstock Craftsman Manual I, II. (Praeger, 1972, 1973) $4.95 each.

List places which teach skills and crafts instruction.

Selling What You Make, by Jane Wood. (Penguin, 1973) $2.25.

Selling Your Crafts, by Norbert N. Nelson. (American Craftsman's Council, 1973) $3.95.

How to Make Money with Your Crafts, by Leta W. Clark. (Morrow, 1974) $7.95.

Vagabonding in America, by Ed Buryn. (Random House-Bookworks, 1973) $4.95.

Somewhere Else: A Living-Learning Catalog. (The Swallow Press, 1139 South Wabash Avenue, Chicago Ill. 60605, revised periodically) $3.00 paper.

Job Exploration:
Volunteering

The Response: Volunteer Service Opportunities. (International Liaison, 39 Lackawanna Place, Bloomfield, N.J. 07003, revised yearly) $1.25.

Working Loose, by the New Vocations Project. (American Friends Service Committee, 2160 Lake Street, San Francisco, Cal. 94121. Also distributed by Random House, 1971) $2.00.

Helping Others, A Guide to Selected Social Service Agencies and Occupations, Norma Haimes, ed. (John Day, 1974) $4.95 paper.
Has a fine bibliography.

Workforce. (Vocations for Social Change, 5951 Canning Street, Oakland, Cal. 94609, a bimonthly magazine). A six-month subscription is $5; a sample copy can be obtained for a donation.
Workforce lists jobs in alternative institutions, educational programs, media, and community organizations.

Job Exploration: Working for Others

Creative Careers for Women: A Handbook of Sources and Ideas for Part-time Jobs, by Joan Scobey and Lee Parr McGrath. (Essandess Special Editions, Simon and Schuster, 1968) $1.00.

The Job Handbook for Postcollege Cop-Outs, by Lawrence Handel. (Pocket Books, 1973) $1.25.

Summer Employment Directory of the U.S., Myrena A. Leith, ed. (National Directory Service, Inc., 266 Ludlow Avenue, Cincinnati, Ohio 45220, revised annually) $5.95 plus a $2.00 February supplement.
Lists summer theaters, camps, restaurants, hotels, amusement parks, national park concessions, and other job opportunities. (This publisher also issues a yearly guide, *Overseas Summer Jobs.*)

World-Wide Summer Placement Directory. (Advancement and Placement Institute, 169 North 9 Street, Brooklyn, N.Y., revised annually) $10.00.

Summer Jobs in Federal Agencies. (U.S. Civil Service
Commission, Washington, D.C. 20415, issued each November) free.

Lists jobs in such agencies as the Bureau of Land
Management, the National Park Service, and the Veterans Administration. Read early; application for summer jobs should be made by Christmas of the year
previous.

Work When You Want to Work, by John Fanning with
George Sullivan. (Collier Books, 1969) $1.25.

Introduces the temporary job scene, lists types of
jobs available; written by the president of an office-
temp company.

Job Exploration:
Working Overseas

Statistical Directory of the International Volunteer Service. Revised periodically. (Send $2.25 plus postage to
International Secretariat for Volunteer Service, 10
Chemin de Surville, 1213 Petit-Lancy, Geneva, Switzerland.)

Lists organizations that sponsor volunteers here
and abroad.

International Directory for Youth Interneships. Revised
periodically. (Send $1.00 to International Directory
for Youth Interneships, to U.S. Committee for UNICEF,
331 East 38th Street, New York, N.Y. 10016.)

Lists jobs with the UN and UN-related organizations.

The Whole World Handbook. (Council on International Educational Exchange, distributed by Simon and Schuster) $2.95.

Lists short- and long-term jobs and trainee programs on the six continents, as well as information on national employment regulations and work permits.

Working Abroad. (Council on International Educational Exchange, 777 United Nations Plaza, New York, N.Y. 10017) free.

An annual fact sheet, updates the information in *The Whole World Handbook* (above).

Employment Abroad—Facts and Fallacies. (Send $1.00 to Foreign Commerce, Foreign Policy Department, Chamber of Commerce of the United States, 1615 H Street, N.W., Washington, D.C. 20006).

Federal Jobs Overseas (CS 1.48:BRE 18/2) $.10; and *American Students and Teachers Abroad: Sources of Information About Overseas Study, Teaching, Work and Travel* (HE 5.214:14174) $.45. (Available from the Superintendent of Documents, U.S. Government Printing Office, Washington, D.C. 20420). Ask for the latest revisions, and include the parenthetical numbers when ordering.

Transferring

Directory of College Transfer Information. Carl M. Dye and Gerald B. Flora, ed. (American Schools Association–Simon and Schuster, 1974) $25.00.

Travel: United States and Canada

Vagabonding in America, by Ed Buryn. (Random House–
Bookworks, 1973) $4.95 paper.

Woodall's Trailering Parks and Campgrounds Directory.
(distributed by Simon and Schuster, annual) $5.95
paper.

    Contains checklists, maps, a dumping stations di-
rectory, and exhaustive data on public and private
parks, campgrounds, and trailer parks.

Hostel Guide and Handbook. (American Youth Hostels,
Inc., National Campus, Delaplane, Va. 22025)

    Free if you join American Youth Hostels ($10 a
year if you're over eighteen), or can be purchased for
$1.50. AYH doesn't require student status.

The North American Bicycle Atlas, by Warren Asa
(Crown, 1973) $2.50.

    A bike-route book published by AYH.

The Hitchhiker's Field Manual, by Paul Dimaggio. (Macmillan, 1973) $1.95 paper.

    Lists useful information; originally Dimaggio's honors
thesis at Swarthmore in the sociology of hitchhiking.

*Side of the Road, A Hitchhiker's Guide to the United
States,* by Ben Lobo and Sara Links. (Simon and
Schuster Fireside Book, 1972) $1.95.

Hitchhiker's Handbook, by Tom Grimm. (New American
Library, n.d.) $2.95 paper.

Adventure Trip Guide (Adventure Guides, Inc., 36 East
57th Street, New York, N.Y. 10022, 1972) $2.95.

Lists names, addresses, and prices for joining cattle drives, packhorse treks, ballooning and soaring trips, and other such activities.

Travel: Eating and Sleeping

Mort's Guide to Low-Cost Vacations and Lodgings on College Campuses, USA and Canada, by Mort Barish. (CMG Publications, Inc., P.O. Box 630, Princeton, N.J. 08540, 1974) $3.95 plus $0.50 postage.

Let's Go, the Student Guide to the United States and Canada, Harvard Student Agencies. (Dutton, 1972) $3.95 paper.

Where to Stay—U.S.A., by Marjorie A. Cohen. (Council on International Education Exchange, distributed by Simon and Schuster, 1975–76 edition) $2.95.

Lists inexpensive lodgings like hostels (independent as well as AYH), Y's, campuses, crisis numbers, eateries.

Communes, USA, A Personal Tour, by R. Fairfield. (Penguin Books, 1971) $3.50.

Monthly News of Co-op Communities (North American Student Cooperative Organization, Box 1301, Ann Arbor, Mich. 48106) $2 per year.

Vocations for Social Change has local offices in Oakland, California; Washington, D.C.; Cambridge, Massachusetts; Ithaca, New York; and Rochester, New York; Bellingham, Washington; and Milwaukee, Wisconsin; they're clearinghouses for community-resource information.

Travel: Overseas

Vagabonding in Europe and North Africa, by Ed Buryn
(distributed by Random House–Bookworks, 1973)
$3.95 paper.

Let's Go: The Student Guide to Europe 1975–76, by
Harvard Student Agencies. (Dutton, 1975) $3.95.

Student Hostels and Restaurants, by Swiss Student Travel
Office. (Available from Council on International Educational Exchange, 777 UN Plaza, New York, N.Y.)
$1.00.

Covers thirty-five countries.

Charter Flights. For brochures, listings, guides, travel
bookings, and charter flight information, check with:
Council on International Educational Exchange
777 United Nations Plaza
New York, N.Y. 10017, or

235 East Santa Clara Street #710
San Jose, Cal. 95113
(Ask for their free *Student Travel Catalog.*)

SOFA (European Student Travel Center)
136 East 57 Street
Suite 1205
New York, N.Y. 10022
(Offers free *Student Travel Guide.*)

Travel-Study

*Whole World Handbook: Six Continents on a Student
Budget* (Council on International Educational Ex-

change–Frommer; distributed by Simon and Schuster, 1974–75 edition) $3.50.

Lists hundreds of accredited programs, *some open to students who've stopped out and are unaffiliated with any college.* Quotes fees, application deadlines, and specific addresses, and includes data about the discounts available with your ISIC.

The Institute of International Education (809 UN Plaza, New York, N.Y. 10017) has a counseling division that will help you arrange study abroad. It also publishes three volumes which, together, will tell you everything you need to know about study opportunities in foreign colleges and universities:

Handbook of International Study for U.S. Nationals covers the year-round and summer-study academic programs open to U.S. citizens in 120 countries, and information on scholarships and awards for overseas study. (1970) $7.00.

Handbook on Study in Europe for U.S. Nationals updates the above volume and includes just the countries of Europe. (1975) $6.95.

U.S. College-Sponsored Programs Abroad describes academic-year programs, travel-study plans, and summer-study opportunities for undergraduates. (revised annually) $3.50.

Guide to Study in Europe—A Selective Guide to European Schools and Universities, by Shirley Yvonne Herman. (Four Winds Press, 1969) $4.25 paper.

Lists hosts of scholarships with where-to-write information.

Two helpful pamphlets are available from the Superintendent of Documents, U.S. Government Printing Office, Washington, D.C. 20402:

Study Abroad (#HE 5.214:14153) 15¢.

Research, Study, Travel and Work Abroad (#HE-14: 14157) 15¢.

Bibliography

The bibliography is ordered by chapter. However, several sources occur in more than one section. In these cases, full references are given only at the first instance; thereafter the author's last name and a shortened title are used.

Chapter 1

BIRD, CAROLINE. *The Case Against College.* New York: David McKay, 1975.

BIRD, CAROLINE, AND NECEL, STEPHEN G. "College: Dumbest Investment of All," in *Esquire,* September 1974.

BOYER, ERNEST L. "Changing Dimensions in Higher Education." In *College Board Review,* Spring 1973.

BREWSTER, KINGMAN, JR. "Colleges Encouraging a Year's Dropout." In *The New York Times,* August 11, 1974, IV, 9.

CARNEGIE COMMISSION ON HIGHER EDUCATION. *Less Time, More Options: Education Beyond High School.* New York: McGraw-Hill, 1971.

————. *Priorities for Action: Final Report of the Carnegie Commission.* New York: McGraw-Hill, 1973.

CROSS, K. PATRICIA. "The Learning Society." In *College Board Review*, Spring 1974.

ESTY, JOHN C., JR. "College Dropouts' Real Problem: What to Drop Into?" In *College Board Review*, Winter 1966–67.

FRANKLIN, BENJAMIN. "The Savages of North America." In *The Works of Benjamin Franklin.* New York: Putnam, 1904.

GUMMERE, RICHARD N. *How to Survive Education.* New York: Harcourt, Brace, Jovanovich, 1971.

HETHERINGTON, FRANK W. "Recruiting by Direct Mail." In *College Board Review*, Spring 1974.

JENKINS, EVAN. "Colleges Shift to Hard Sell in Recruiting Students." In *The New York Times*, March 31, 1974, I, 1.

KENISTON, KENNETH. *Youth and Dissent, the Rise of a New Opposition.* New York: Harcourt, Brace, Jovanovich, 1971.

LINDAHL, CHARLES W. "But Is Recruiting Really Obsolete?" In *College Board Review*, Fall 1973.

MOOD, ALEXANDER M. *The Future of Higher Education—Some Speculations and Suggestions.* The Carnegie Commission on Higher Education. New York: McGraw-Hill, 1973.

PERVIN, LAWRENCE A.; REIK, LOUIS E.; AND DALRYMPLE, WILLARD, eds. *The College Dropout and the Utilization of Talent.* Princeton, N.J.: Princeton University Press, 1966.

RAPOPORT, ROGER. "New Myth On Campus." In *Esquire,* September 1974.

TAUBMAN, PAUL, AND WALES, TERENCE. *Mental Ability and Higher Educational Attainment in the Twentieth Century.* Carnegie Commission on Higher Education.

TINTO, VINCENT, AND CULLEN, JOHN. *Dropout in Higher Education: A Review and Theoretical Synthesis of Recent Research.* ERIC Document Reproduction Service, ED 078 802, 1973.

VERMILYE, DYCKMAN W., ed. *The Expanded Campus.* San Francisco: Jossey-Bass, 1972.

Chapter 2

ASTIN, ALEXANDER W. "College Dropouts: A National Profile." American Council on Education. ERIC Document Reproduction Service, ED 059 691, 1972.

————. *Preventing Students from Dropping Out* (tentative title). San Francisco: Jossey-Bass, forthcoming.

"As College Starts, There Go the Stopouts." *Time,* September 27, 1971.

BABBOTT, EDWARD F. "Postponing College; Alternatives for an Interim Year." In *College Board Review,* Summer 1971.

BARD, BERNARD. "College Students: Why They Drop Out." In *Kiwanis,* September 1968.

BEHRENS, DAVID. "Students on Sabbatical." In *Newsday,* November 22, 1974.

BLAI, BORIS, JR. "Two-Year College Dropouts—Why Do They Leave? Who Are They? How Many?" ERIC Document Reproduction Service, ED 058 879, 1972.

BROZAN, NADINE. "Widening Gap in Views Is Registered Between College and Non-College Women." In *The New York Times*, May 22, 1974.

CARNEGIE COMMISSION, *Less Time, More Options.*

———. *Priorities for Action.*

———. *The Purposes and Performances of Higher Education in the United States Approaching the Year 2000.* New York: McGraw-Hill, 1973.

CLIFFORD, MARGARET M., AND WALSTER, ELAINE. "The Effect of Sex on College Admissions, Work Evaluation and Job Interviews." In *Journal of Experimental Education,* Winter 1972.

EAGLE, NORMAN. "Dropout Prediction at an Urban Community College Following Open Admissions." ERIC Document Reproduction Service, ED 073 753, 1973.

ESTY, "College Dropouts' Real Problem: What to Drop Into?"

FLANNERY, JOHN, et al. "Final Report for the Ad Hoc Committee to Study Attrition at Miami-Dade Community College, North Campus." ERIC Document Reproduction Service, ED 085 052, 1973.

GRAZIANO, A. F. "Dropout Survey at the University of Illinois Urbana Campus." ERIC Document Reproduction Service, ED 078 750, 1971.

GROSS, RONALD. "After Deschooling, Free Learning." In *Social Policy,* January–February 1972.

GUMMERE, *How to Survive Education.*

HECHINGER, FRED M. "Youth's New Values." In *The New York Times,* May 28, 1974, p. 39.

HEIST, PAUL, ed. *The Creative College Student: An Unmet Challenge.* San Francisco: Jossey-Bass, 1968.

KAMENS, DAVID H. "The Effect of College on Student Dropout—Final Report." ERIC Document Reproduction Service, ED 068 038, 1972.

KENISTON, KENNETH. "Youth: A New Stage of Life." In *The American Scholar,* August 1970.

MEHRA, N. "Retention and Withdrawal of University Students." ERIC Document Reproduction Service, ED 087 296, 1973.

MOOD, *The Future of Higher Education.*

NEWMAN, FRANK, et al. *Report on Higher Education.* Office of Education, U.S. Department of Health, Education and Welfare, March 1971.

NICHOLSON, E. "Predictors of Graduation from College." ERIC Document Reproduction Service, ED 076 153, 1973.

NOMER, HOWELL F. "Do Most Students Need 'Time Out' Between School and College?" In *College Board Review,* Spring 1968.

PANDEY, R. E. "Comparative Study of Dropouts at an Integrated University." In *Journal of Negro Education,* Fall 1973.

PITCHER, ROBERT W., AND BLAUSCHILD, BABETTE. *Why College Students Fail.* New York: Funk and Wagnalls, 1970.

PERVIN, *The College Dropout.*

RALSTON, NANCY C., AND THOMAS, PATIENCE. "America's Artificial Adolescents." In *Adolescence,* Spring 1972.

ROGERS, CARL R. *Freedom to Learn*. Columbus, Ohio: Merrill, 1969.

TAUBMAN AND WALES, *Mental Ability and Higher Educational Attainment*.

TINTO AND CULLEN, *Dropout in Higher Education*.

TRENT, JAMES W., AND MEDSKER, LELAND L. *Beyond High School*. San Francisco: Jossey-Bass, 1968.

VERMILYE, *The Expanded Campus*.

WHARTON, WILLIAM P. "In Defense of Dropping Out." In *College Board Review*, Summer 1966.

WHITTAKER, DAVID A. "The Psychological Adjustment of Intellectual, Non-conformist, Collegiate Dropouts." In *Adolescence*, VI, 24.

WILLETT, LYNN H. "Non-Persisting Student Follow-up." ERIC Document Reproduction Service, ED 078 821, 1973.

WILLINGHAM, WARREN W., AND FINDIKYAN, NURHAN, "Transfer Students: Who's Moving from Where to Where, and What Determines Who's Admitted?" In *College Board Review*, Summer 1969.

Unpublished Reports

"A Report on Voluntary Withdrawals from Wheaton 1973–74." Wheaton College, Massachusetts, 1974.

"A Study of Voluntary Student Withdrawals from Wheaton 1972–73." Wheaton College, Massachusetts, 1973.

BLAI, BORIS, JR. "Sustained Student 'Holding Power' at Harcum." Harcum Junior College, Pennsylvania, 1971.

COLLINS, ISABEL. Interview re dissertation in progress. Columbia University, N.Y., 1975.

HAAGEN, C. HESS. Interview re untitled six-college stopout survey in progress. Wesleyan University, Connecticut, 1975.

JASS, RUTH. "Survey of Full-time Students Who Indicated They Would Not Enroll at Bradley for the Fall Semester 1971–72." Bradley University, Illinois, 1971.

———. "Survey of Non-Enrollees for 1972." Bradley University, Illinois, 1973.

KESTER, DONALD L. "California Community College Stopouts: A Comparision of the Three Nor-Cal-CCHE Follow-Up Studies." California State Coordinating Council for Higher Education and Northern California Community College Research Group, 1971.

LINDSAY, NANCY SILVER. "Where Did You Go? Out!" Harvard University, Massachusetts, 1974.

SCHELL, ROBERT E. "Trends and Projections of Voluntary Student Withdrawls at SUNY/Oswego; 1967–1976." State University of New York at Oswego, New York, 1973.

SPARKS, LOIS R. "Who Withdraws from Antioch?" Antioch College, Ohio, 1973.

"Undergraduate Withdrawal from Vanderbilt College of Original Entry." Vanderbilt College, Tennessee, 1974.

YARTZ, LARRY J. "Student Attrition at Allegheny College." Allegheny College, Pennsylvania, 1974.

Chapter 3

BABBOTT, EDWARD F. "A Year Early: What 378 Colleges Say About Admitting Students Right After Their Junior

Year of High School." In *College Board Review*, Spring 1973.

———. "Postponing College."

Barron's Profiles of American Colleges: Volume 2. Barron's Educational Series, 1973.

CARNEGIE COMMISSION, *Priorities for Action.*

COPE, ROBERT, AND WILLIAM HANNAH, *Revolving College Doors*, John Wiley and Sons, 1975.

"Early Admissions," pamphlet of Five Towns College, Merrick, Long Island, 1974.

ECKLAND, B. K. "College Dropouts Who Came Back." In *Harvard Educational Review*, Spring 1964.

"Futurist Eurich Addresses Members." In *Communique*, Summer 1972.

KESTER, DONALD L., "California Community College Stopouts."

LINDSAY, "Where Did You Go? Out!"

MACMITCHELL, T. LESLIE. "Stopout: A College and University Survey." In *College Board Review*, Winter 1972–73.

MOOD, *The Future of Higher Education.*

NEWMAN, *Report on Higher Education.*

NOMER, *"Do Most Students Need 'Time Out'?"*

Providing Optional Learning Environments in New York State Schools. State Education Department, University of the State of New York, 1973.

WHITE, DARREL K. "AP Year in Utah." In *College Board Review*, Fall 1974.

YARTZ, "Student Attrition at Allegheny College."

Chapter 4

BOK, DEREK C. "Greetings to the Conference Participants." In *Changing Patterns for Undergraduate Education*, report on a conference sponsored by the College Entrance Examination Board and Harvard University. College Entrance Examination Board, 1972.

BOYER, "Changing Dimensions in Higher Education."

CARNEGIE COMMISSION, *Less Time, More Options.*

————. *Priorities for Action.*

LIVESEY, HERBERT B., AND ROBBINS, GENE A. *Guide to American Graduate Schools*, second edition. New York: Viking Press, 1970.

NEWMAN, *Report on Higher Education.*

"Professionals Here Find Market for Jobs is Tight." In *The New York Times*, September 1, 1974, p. 1.

RAPOPORT, "New Myth on Campus."

"Small But Growing Number of Colleges Across Nation Adopting A Year-Round, Three-Term Program." In *The New York Times*, August 23, 1973, p. 21.

The Top Ten. Pamphlet of the State University of New York, 1974.

"The Whys and Why-Nots of Going Through College in Three Years." In *Seventeen*, August 1973.

Chapter 5

"A Selected List of Major Fellowship Opportunities and Aids to Advanced Education for U.S. Citizens." National Academy of Sciences, 1974.

ASTIN, "College Dropouts."

"A Study of Voluntary Withdrawals from Wheaton, 1972–73."

BEHRENS, "Students on Sabbatical."

BLAI, "Sustained Student 'Holding Power.'"

BREWSTER, "Colleges Encouraging a Year's Dropout."

"Five Federal Financial Aid Programs." Department of Health, Education and Welfare, 1974.

HAAGEN, C. HESS, "Progress Report, Survey 1, January 1974." Typewritten. Wesleyan University, 1974.

————. "Progress Report #2, 'Leave-Taking' Study: Cooperative Research Project." Typewritten. Wesleyan University, 1974.

LEVINE, JOEL, AND MAY, LAWRENCE. *Getting In, A Guide to Acceptance at the College of Your Choice.* New York: Random House, 1972.

LINDSAY, "Where Did You Go? Out!"

MOOD, *The Future of Higher Education.*

NEWMAN, *Report on Higher Education.*

NOMER, "Do Most Students Need 'Time Out'?"

PERVIN, *The College Dropout.*

REINHOLD, ROBERT. "At Brown, Trend Is Back to Grades and Tradition." In *The New York Times,* February 23, 1974, p. 6.

ROONEY, RICHARD D. "Guidelines Suggest Ways to Help Transfer Students." In *College Board Review,* Spring 1974.

TINTO AND CULLEN, *Dropout in Higher Education.*

WARNER, RAY. "College, at Early Opening, Stresses Parent's Role." In *The New York Times,* August 25, 1974, p. 39.

WHARTON, "In Defense of Dropping Out."

WILLINGHAM AND FINDIKYAN, "Transfer Students."

WOODRING, PAUL. *Who Should Go to College?* Phi Delta Kappa Foundation, 1972.

Chapter 6

COLEMAN, JOHN R. *Blue-Collar Journal: A College President's Sabbatical.* Philadelphia: Lippincott, 1974.

COPE AND HANNAH. *Revolving College Doors.*

GUMMERE, RICHARD N. "DIG/Columbia University's Program to Help Students Find Answers." In *Journal of College Placement*, April–May 1972.

LINDSAY, "Where Did You Go? Out!"

MILLER, GORDON P., AND GELATT, H. B. "Deciding: The Decision-Making Program." In *College Board Review*, Winter 1971–72.

NATIONAL INSTITUTES OF MENTAL HEALTH. *Facts About College Mental Health.* Washington, D.C.: U.S. Government Printing Office: (HSM)72-9154, 1972.

Chapter 7

"A Report on Voluntary Withdrawals from Wheaton 1973–74."

"A Study of Voluntary Student Withdrawals from Wheaton."

ROGERS, *Freedom to Learn.*

Chapter 8

COLEMAN, Blue-Collar Journal.

WALLACH, MICHAEL A., AND WING, CLIFF W., JR. *The Talented Students—A Validity of the Creativity-Intelligence Distinction.* New York: Holt, Rinehart and Winston, 1969.

WHITE, G. *"Functional Resume."* Mimeographed. Washington Opportunities for Women. 1974.

Chapter 9

The Advantage of Work-Study Plans, Management Division, Academy for Educational Development. Academy for Educational Development, n.d.

CROSS, "The Learning Society."

KNOWLES, ASA S. *A College President Looks at Cooperative Education,* occasional paper. National Commission for Cooperative Education, 1964.

NEWMAN, FRANK, et al. *Second Report on Higher Education.* Office of Education, Department of Health, Education and Welfare, 1974.

Chapter 10

BABBOTT, "Postponing College."

BOLLES, RICHARD NELSON. *What Color Is Your Parachute?* Berkeley, Cal.: Ten Speed Press, 1972.

DRESSEL, PAUL L., AND THOMPSON, MARY M. *Independent Study.* San Francisco: Jossey-Bass, 1973.

JAROSLOVSKY, RICH. "Live and Learn: Home Study Leaves Some People Sadder and Maybe No Wiser." In the *Wall Street Journal,* December 31, 1974, p. 1.

"Lures of the Trade Schools." In *The New York Times,* December 22, 1974, IV, 5.

MAYHEW, LEWIS B. "Can Undergraduate Independent Study Courses Succeed?" In *College Board Review,* Spring 1971.

VERMILYE, *The Expanded Campus.*

Chapter 11

CASSERLY, PATRICIA LUND. "What College Students Say About Advanced Placement." In *College Board Review,* Fall 1968, Winter 1968–69.

CHRIST-JANER, ARLAND F., in Vermilye, *The Expanded Campus.*

CLEP May Be for You. College Entrance Examination Board, 1974.

DRESSEL AND THOMPSON, *Independent Study.*

HOULE, CYRIL O. *The External Degree.* San Francisco: Jossey-Bass, 1973.

SUMMERSKILL, JOHN. "Non-Traditional Education: Fundamental Change or Passing Fad?" In *Vital Issues,* November 1972.

VALLEY, JOHN R. *Increasing the Options: Recent Developments in College and University Degree Programs.* Office of New Degree Programs. College Entrance Examination Board and Educational Testing Service, 1972.

WHITAKER, URBAN. "A Case Study of CLEP: Credit by Examination at San Francisco State College." In *College Board Review,* Spring 1972.

Chapter 12

CARNEGIE COMMISSION ON HIGHER EDUCATION. *Breaking the Access Barrier.* New York: McGraw-Hill.

———. *The Purposes and Performances of Higher Education.*

GUMMERE, *How to Survive Education.*

KEATS, JUHN. *The Sheepskin Psychosis.* Philadelphia: Lippincott, 1965.

MCLAUGHLIN, GERALD W. "Pass-Fail Grading." In the *Journal of Experimental Education,* Fall 1972.

MAYHEW, LEWIS B. *The Carnegie Commission on Higher Education: A Critical Analysis of the Reports and Recommendations.* San Francisco: Jossey-Bass, 1973.

MOOD, *The Future of Higher Education.*

NEWMAN, *Report on Higher Education.*

SUMMERSKILL, "Non-Traditional Education."

TRENT AND MEDSKER, *Beyond High School.*

Index